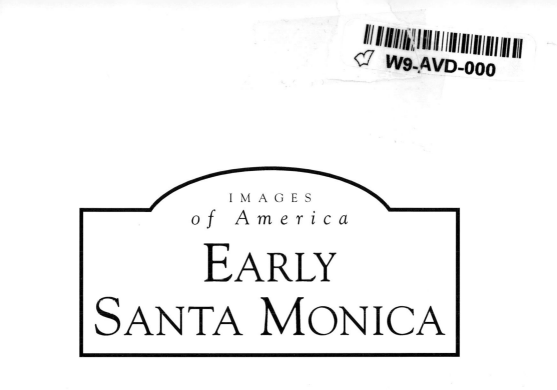

IMAGES
of America

EARLY
SANTA MONICA

Louise B. Gabriel
Santa Monica Historical Society Museum

ARCADIA
PUBLISHING

Published by Arcadia Publishing
Charleston, South Carolina

Printed in the United States of America

Library of Congress Catalog Card Number: 2006923164

For all general information contact Arcadia Publishing at:
Telephone 843-853-2070
Fax 843-853-0044
E-mail sales@arcadiapublishing.com
For customer service and orders:
Toll-Free 1-888-313-2665

Visit us on the Internet at www.arcadiapublishing.com

I would like to dedicate this book to Santa Monica's cofounders, Col. Robert S. Baker and Sen. John P. Jones, whose vision and foresight paved the way for the beautiful city Santa Monica is today; to my husband, Bob, and family for all their wonderful support; and to the Santa Monica Historical Society Museum, Santa Monica's treasure, and its dedicated staff, board of directors, and supporters.

CONTENTS

ACKNOWLEDGMENTS

My involvement in the history of Santa Monica began when I served on the Historical Activities Committee of the Santa Monica Centennial Committee in 1975. I had the opportunity to meet and get to know many descendants of the cofounders of the city and early pioneers and to hear firsthand their families' histories.

It was during the centennial that the Santa Monica Historical Society was founded. I founded the museum in 1988.

I feel honored to author this book with images that give a visual history of Santa Monica's past. Most all of them are from the Santa Monica Historical Society Museum's extensive archives.

Special thanks to my husband, Bob, and family for their patience and wonderful support while I was writing this book. My thanks to Jerry Roberts of Arcadia Publishing for his helpful guidance.

I am grateful for the photographs used from the museum's collections and to those who provided them, namely, the *Outlook* newspaper, Bill Beebe, Bob Smith, Elliott Welsh, Herb Roney, Santa Monica–Malibu Unified School District, Jane Newcomb Whiting, Ricardo Bandini Johnson, John Farquhar, Marc Wanamaker, and Bison Archives.

My thanks and appreciation to our Santa Monica Historical Society Museum staff members Dr. Andrea Engstrom and Ho Nguyen for their valuable technical help in scanning images and materials and to the volunteers who assisted, including Dona Snow, Jo Cherkas, Rosita Mal, Rebekah Drew, Ivana Mladenovic, Allen Frankel, Anna Lisa DeBois, John Sullivan, Dina Murokh, Cody Kennedy, Andrea Linares, and Brenda Koplin.

Visit our web site at www.santamonicahistory.org.

INTRODUCTION

Throughout its history, Santa Monica has been described by many endearing phrases, among them "City by the Sea," "Pearl of the Pacific," "City of Inspiration," and "Jewel of the Sunset Bay." With an environment of mountains, canyons, rolling hills, valleys, and ocean, and blessed with a delightful all-year climate, industry, commerce, and the arts, Santa Monica has its high place in the world. It is a place to live and enjoy life. As it was with the Gabrielino and Chumash Indians who dwelt here before the Spanish explorers discovered the area, so it shall ever be.

In 1542, Juan Rodriquez Cabrillo, a Spanish conquistador, dropped anchor in what is thought to be Santa Monica Bay. In 1769, Spanish explorer Gaspar de Portola was placed in command of an expedition in California. While Portola and his party rested in camp, some of the men hunted for a trail up the coast. As the story goes, it was hot and dusty as the little party walked over the pathless plain. They came to two springs of sparkling water below a shade of great sycamore trees. After drinking the cool water and resting in the shade, the little party agreed that this place should have a name. The day, May 4, happened to be St. Monica's day on the religious calendar, and as the springs reminded them of the tears St. Monica shed for her erring son Augustine, they called the area Santa Monica.

In 1822, the land passed from Spanish rule to the Mexican Republic and came under private ownership. In 1828, Don Francisco Sepulveda was given provisional title to Rancho San Vicente y Santa Monica, which included the area between the Santa Monica Canyon and what is now Pico Boulevard and northeasterly into the Westwood region. In 1839, Ysidro Reyes and Francisco Marquez were provisionally granted the rancho known as Boca de Santa Monica (Santa Monica Canyon).

During the gold rush days of 1849, Col. Robert S. Baker came from Rhode Island to San Francisco and went into business selling mining supplies and raising cattle in the Tejon country. Looking for more grazing land for his livestock, he purchased the Rancho San Vicente y Santa Monica from the Don Francisco Sepulveda heirs in 1872 for $55,000.

Colonel Baker began to talk of a town on the bay. He believed that Southern California was sure to grow into a thriving, prosperous region. Colonel Baker knew it would take a great deal of money to make this happen, so he tried to interest some eastern capitalists in investing their money. In 1874, wealthy U.S. senator John P. Jones of Nevada came to California. He purchased three-fourths interest in Colonel Baker's ranch for $162,500. Colonel Baker and Senator Jones began making plans for a town, believing it was going to become "the great commercial center of the Southwest."

On July 10, 1875, a town site plat was filed with the county recorder. On July 15, 1875, the first lots were put on the auction block, which sold from $75 to $500. Tom Fitch, the auctioneer, made an eloquent speech that had a great impression on the bidders. "At one o'clock we will sell at public outcry to the highest bidder the Pacific Ocean, draped with a western sky of scarlet and gold; we will sell a bay filled with white winged ships; we will sell a southern horizon, rimmed with a choice collection of purple mountains carved in castles and turrets and domes; we will sell a frostless, bracing, warm yet unlangured air braided in and out with sunshine and odored with the breath of flowers." Listening to the speeches, people became anxious to own a lot in the new town. They forgot the dusty, barren plain.

Within a few weeks after the town lot sale, a change came over the barren plain. Houses and stores sprang up, a general store was opened, and a newspaper started.

Although some of Colonel Baker's and Senator Jones's dreams materialized, they were disappointed that the harbor at Santa Monica was not the one chosen by Los Angeles for the Los Angeles Port and that Santa Monica was not a commercial city. In later years, the residents were glad that the beautiful bay and mountain country did not become an industrial or commercial region. In November 1886, the city electorate went to the polls and voted 97 to 71 to incorporate Santa Monica.

In 1905, the town had a population of 7,208. By the 1920s, the population was growing rapidly. The Ocean Park and Venice pleasure piers drew huge crowds, as did the Looff Pier (Santa Monica Pier). The northern area of Santa Monica had become a renowned resort for the rich and famous, and many lived along the Gold Coast. There were numerous sports enthusiasts. From 1909 to 1919, thrilling road races that began on Ocean Avenue were watched by thousands of people. This, and tennis, put Santa Monica in the national limelight. In 1924, the first round-the-world flight was made in Donald Douglas–built World Cruisers. The flight put Santa Monica on the map. The city struggled during the 1930s Depression and the 1940s war years, but the late 1940s and 1950s were prosperous for Santa Monica as its population soared to more than 83,000. From its very beginning, Santa Monica has been world renowned as a place of leisure, tourism, scenic splendor, and year-round fun.

One

A Town Is Born

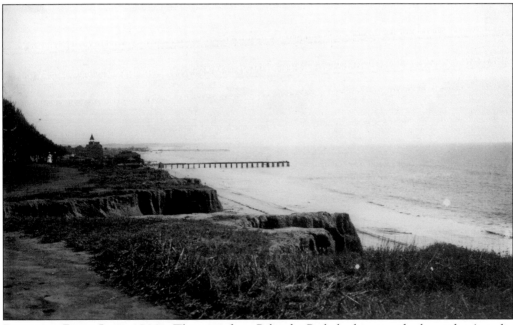

PALISADES PARK, LATE 1800S. This view from Palisades Park, looking south, shows the Arcadia Hotel. When Santa Monica Bay was first discovered in 1542 by Spanish explorer Juan Cabrillo, it was inhabited by the Chumash Indians in the Malibu area and Gabrielinos where West Los Angeles is today. In 1828, Don Francisco Sepulveda owned the Santa Monica area. The land was used for cattle and sheep grazing. In 1872, Col. Robert S. Baker purchased the property from the Sepulveda heirs and soon after, with his business partner, Sen. John P. Jones, founded the town of Santa Monica. (Santa Monica Historical Society Museum, Jones Collection.)

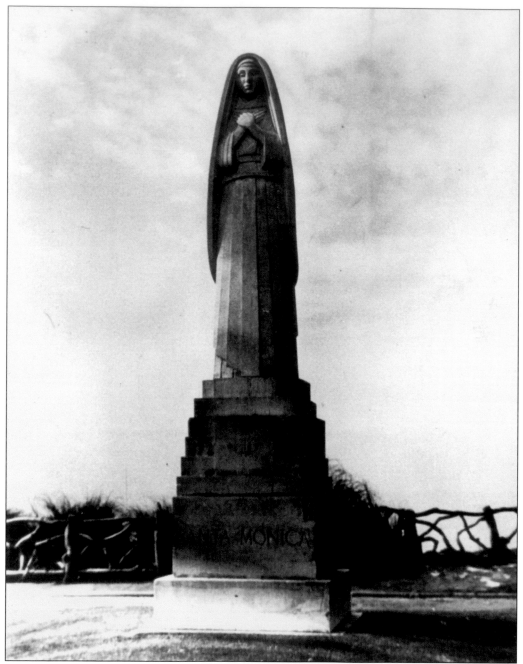

STATUE OF ST. MONICA. Situated at the foot of Wilshire Boulevard, this statue is a symbol of the city. It was sculpted in 1934 by Eugene H. Morahan as a Federal Arts Project. The legend of the city's name has it that on May 4, 1769, Spanish soldiers exploring the area stopped to refresh themselves at a spring near the present area of West Los Angeles. The day happened to be St. Monica's Day on the religious calendar, and as the spring reminded them of the tears St. Monica shed for her erring son, Augustine, they called the area Santa Monica. (Courtesy Dorothy Baker.)

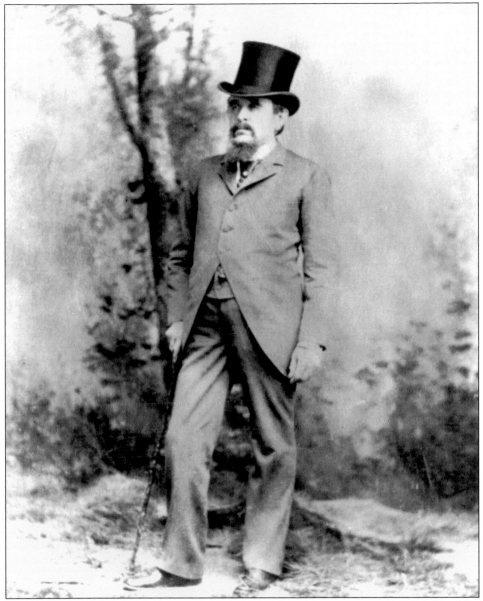

COL. ROBERT SYMINGTON BAKER, COFOUNDER OF SANTA MONICA, C. 1874. Colonel Baker, originally from Rhode Island, came to California in 1849 during the gold rush and engaged in business in San Francisco dealing in mining supplies. Later he was in the cattle and sheep business. In 1872, Colonel Baker purchased the Rancho San Vicente y Santa Monica from the Don Francisco Sepulveda heirs for $55,000. He then began to think of starting a town on the land and sought a wealthy investor. He soon found a partner by the name of Sen. John P. Jones. Colonel Baker married Arcadia Bandini Stearns, a widow, in 1874. In 1878, he built the Baker block in Los Angeles, the finest business block in the city at that time. Colonel Baker was quiet in his tastes and made no effort to enter into public life but donated his time to the management of his large interests. He was most congenial in character, and he and his wife, Arcadia, were noted for their lavish entertainment of guests. They were hosts to many distinguished people. Colonel Baker died in May 1894.

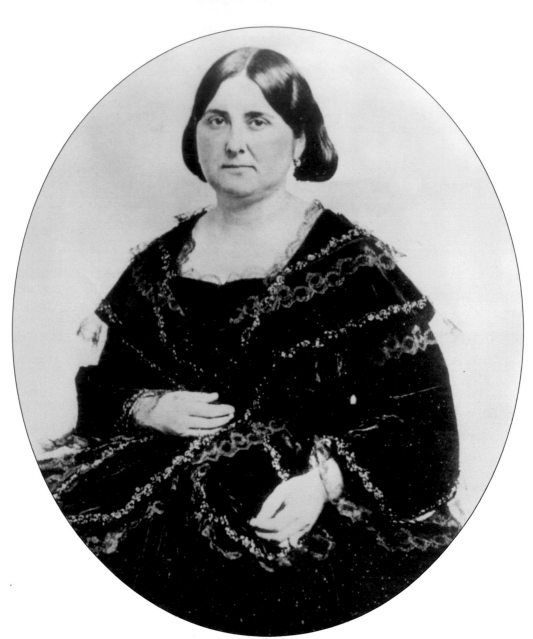

ARCADIA BANDINI STEARNS DE BAKER. Arcadia Bandini de Baker was the daughter of Juan Bandini, one of the wealthiest landowners in California. She married Col. Robert S. Baker in 1874. In their home, she reigned as queen over the rich and famous, politicians, and world figures. The Bakers had no children. Arcadia purchased her husband's holdings on February 4, 1879, for business and personal reasons, and she became a business partner of Sen. John P. Jones. Together they donated land for schools, churches, and parks, including the Palisades Park, then called Linda Vista Park. Arcadia wore exquisite gowns of crepe and silk and satin shoes on her feet. She enjoyed good jewelry and wore it most becomingly. Her hair was fashioned high on her head with a large comb. Whenever she went outdoors, she wore a lovely lace mantilla over her head and a scarf about her shoulders. After her husband's death, she lived in a modest cottage on Ocean Avenue. Arcadia died in September 1912.

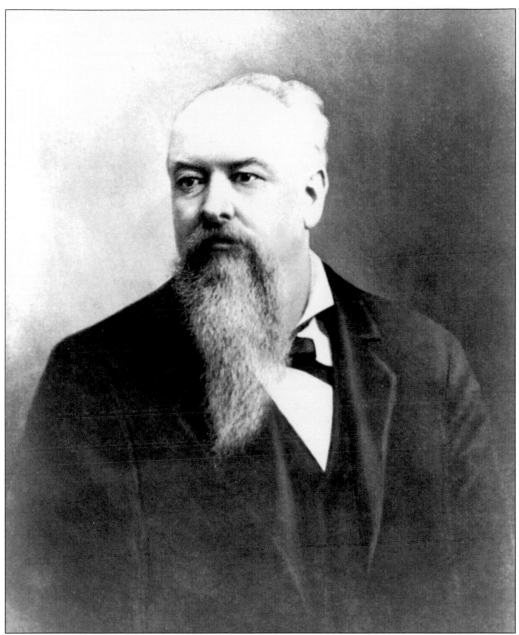

SEN. JOHN PERCIVAL JONES, COFOUNDER OF SANTA MONICA, C. 1875. Originally from England, Senator Jones, a multimillionaire from silver and gold mining in Nevada, came to Santa Monica in 1874 and purchased three-fourths of Colonel Baker's property for $162,500. Together they founded the town of Santa Monica on July 10, 1875. Senator Jones, a widower with a young son, Roy, married Georgina Sullivan in 1875. The family residence, known as Miramar, was a center for entertainment and celebrated throughout the country for its hospitality to men and women of achievement in every field, including statesmen, artists, and notables such as Mark Twain. In his younger years, Senator Jones served as sheriff of Trinity County, California, and was later elected to the state legislature. In 1873, he became a U.S. senator for Nevada and served for 30 years. He died in 1912. (Santa Monica Historical Society Museum, Jones Collection.)

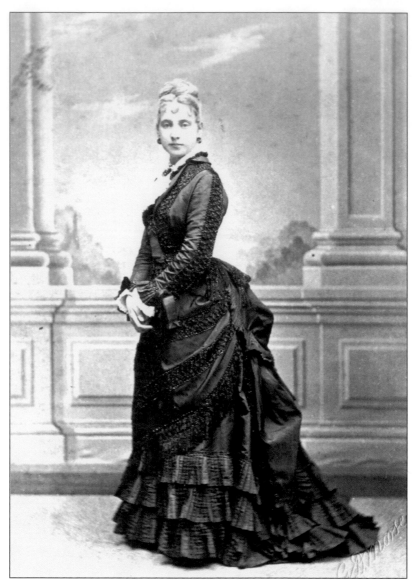

GEORGINA SULLIVAN JONES, 1875. Georgina Jones was the wife of Sen. John P. Jones. Her father was the honorable Eugene L. Sullivan, collector of the port of San Francisco. Georgina and the senator had three daughters, Alice, Marion, and Georgina. She was described as a very warm and gracious person. She and her husband resided in their home, Miramar, from 1891 to 1912. The Miramar was a three-story Victorian house with 17 bedrooms, a huge living room, dining room, kitchen, smoking room, and library. It also had a smaller dining room for the servants and children, who ate earlier than the rest of the family. A great-aunt ran the house with the aid of five or six servants, a gardener, and a liveryman. Three cows were kept in a corral, providing milk for the family daily, and chickens supplied fresh eggs. Pigs and horses were also kept on the property. The youngsters enjoyed tennis, basketball, and croquet at facilities on the Miramar grounds. The grounds also had a Moreton Bay fig tree, which still stands where the Fairmont Miramar Hotel is today on Wilshire Boulevard and Ocean Avenue. The Jones family sold Miramar in 1912. The senator died the same year. Following his death, Georgina moved to New York where she died in 1936. (Santa Monica Historical Society Museum, Jones Collection.)

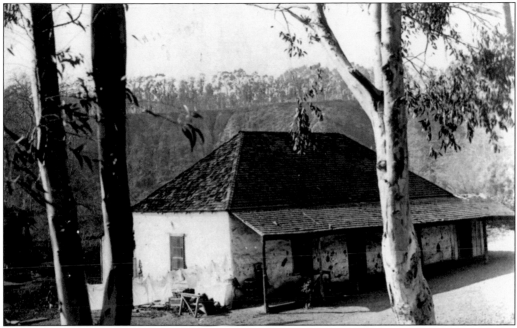

THE MARQUEZ ADOBE, C. 1925. The Marquez adobe in Santa Monica Canyon, along with the Reyes house, was the first built in that area. The adobe collapsed during the 1933 earthquake. Francisco Marquez and Ysidro Reyes were given a provisional title to Rancho Boca de Santa Monica (Santa Monica Canyon). The grant was confirmed by Governor Alvarado in 1839. (Courtesy Santa Monica Public Library Image Archives.)

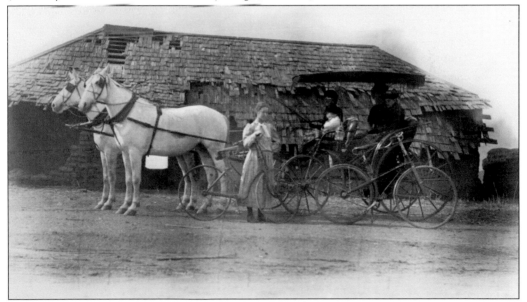

THE REYES ADOBE, C. 1900. Senator Jones's family members are on an outing near Santa Monica's first house, which was built by landowner Ysidro Reyes near Seventh Street and Adelaide Drive. In 1839, Ysidro Reyes and Francisco Marquez were granted the rancho known as Boca de Santa Monica (Santa Monica Canyon). Weathered and crumbling, the adobe building was destroyed in 1906. (Santa Monica Historical Society Museum, Jones Collection.)

15

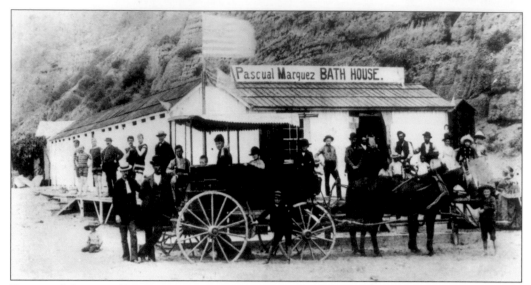

PASCUAL MARQUEZ BATHHOUSE, C. 1880. Santa Monica Canyon's first bathhouse was operated by Pascual Marquez, son of Francisco Marquez, a land grantee of the canyon. It was located just north of the incline where Chautauqua Boulevard is today. Though Michael Duffy built and owned the bathhouse, he named it in honor of Pascual Marquez, who owned the land. The Canyon Bathhouse was built in 1915 on the same site. (Courtesy Santa Monica Public Library Image Archives.)

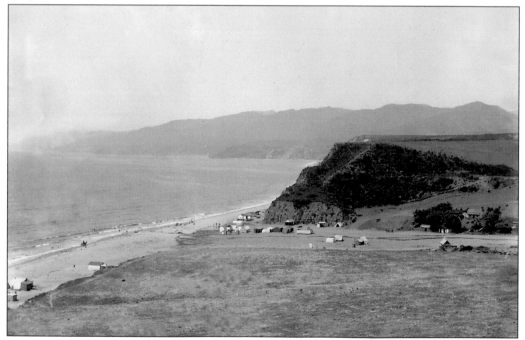

SANTA MONICA CANYON. To escape the heat and dust of Los Angeles, people came to the canyon to camp under big sycamore trees near some springs. The Marquez and Reyes families, who owned the land, welcomed families to camp as long as they wished. By 1915, the number of visitors greatly increased and more vacation shelters were built closer to the beach, as seen in this photograph. (Santa Monica Historical Society Museum, *Outlook* Collection.)

PASCUAL MARQUEZ FAMILY CEMETERY, 1908. The site of the first Marquez house is in the little Spanish cemetery in Santa Monica Canyon. The cemetery was laid out by Pascual Marquez as a family burying ground. In it are buried members of the Marquez and Reyes families and some of their close friends. In 1916, Pascual Marquez was the last person to be buried in this cemetery. (Courtesy Angie Marquez Olivera.)

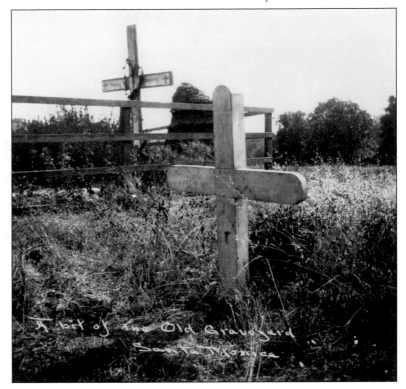

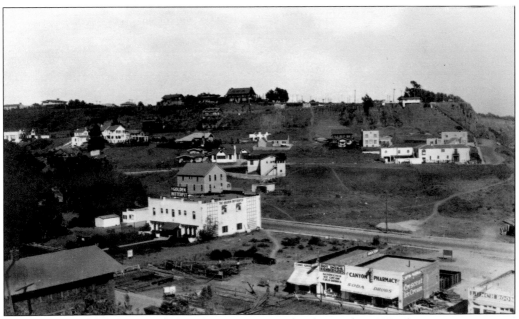

SANTA MONICA CANYON, 1920. The canyon was developing by 1923 when a grocery store, Doc Law's Pharmacy, and several cafés opened for business. There was also an apartment house called the Golden Butterfly.

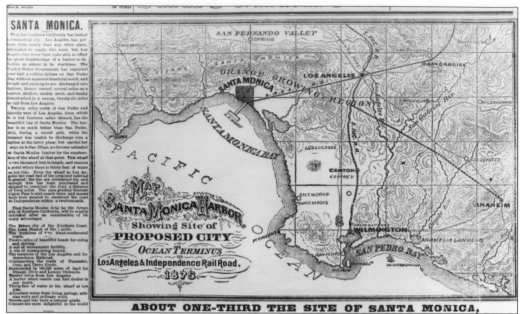

MAP OF SANTA MONICA HARBOR, 1875. Advertisements like this one, published in the San Francisco entertainment paper *Figaro*, helped stir up business for the public auction of lots in Santa Monica on July 15, 1875. Hundreds of San Franciscans made the voyage down the coast aboard two side-wheel steamers for the first subdivision sales. (Santa Monica Historical Society Museum, *Outlook* Collection.)

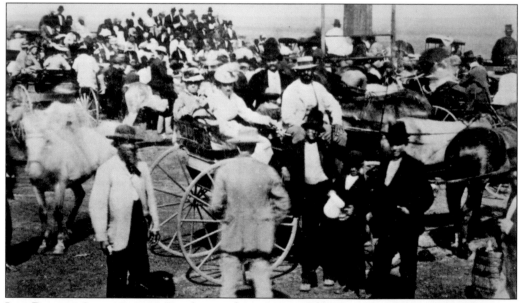

LOT BUYERS, JULY 15, 1875. People came by steamers and horse and buggies to bid on the town of Santa Monica's first land auction. On that hot and dry day, under the spell of the eloquent auctioneer, Tom Fitch, many investors were fired up in the belief that their fortunes were made and all that was required of them was to wait in happy expectation for the day Santa Monica would become the greatest seaport on the Pacific Coast. The lots sold for between $75 and $500. (Courtesy Los Angeles Public Library, Security Pacific Bank Collection.)

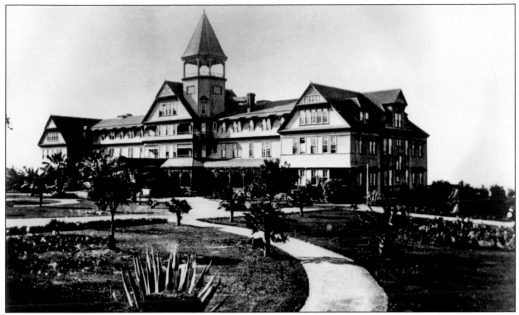

ARCADIA HOTEL, C. 1892. The Arcadia Hotel was one of the most distinguished hotels on the Pacific Coast. It opened in late 1887 and was named for Arcadia Bandini de Baker, the wife of Col. Robert S. Baker, cofounder of Santa Monica. The hotel was located on Ocean Avenue between Railroad Avenue (now Colorado Boulevard) and Front Street (now Pico Boulevard). (Santa Monica Historical Society Museum, *Outlook* Collection.)

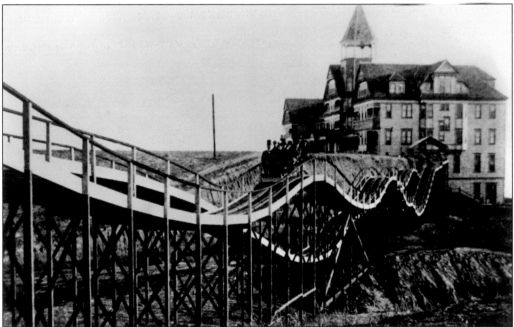

ARCADIA HOTEL COASTER, C. 1890. The hotel was connected to the town across the old railroad gorge by a unique Thompson Switchback Gravity Railroad. It was the forerunner of the roller coaster, and its gentle dips thrilled passengers. It could carry 10 people, and a round-trip ride cost 5¢. (Courtesy Arthur Carrillo Calkins.)

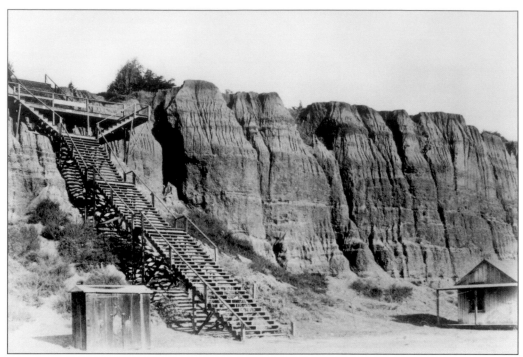

THE 99 STEPS, LATE 1899. This wooden staircase was constructed in 1875 to allow easy access to the beach. It was located at the foot of Arizona Avenue. In 1893, it was altered so that Southern Pacific trains en route to the Long Wharf could pass underneath.

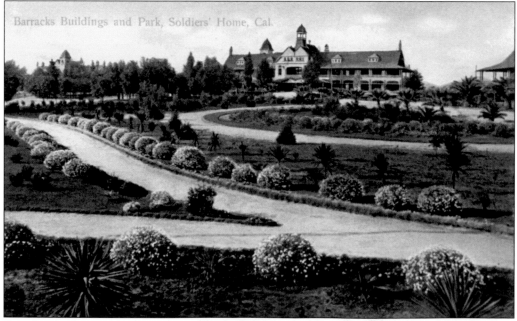

Barracks Buildings and Park, Soldiers' Home, Cal.

SOLDIERS'S HOME. The first national home for veterans west of the Rockies was founded in 1888 on land donated by Sen. John P. Jones and Arcadia Bandini de Baker. It became the Veterans Administration in 1930. Pictured here, the complex of 1892 included military-style barracks, a mess hall, and a recreation center, as well as a theater, library, and chapel.

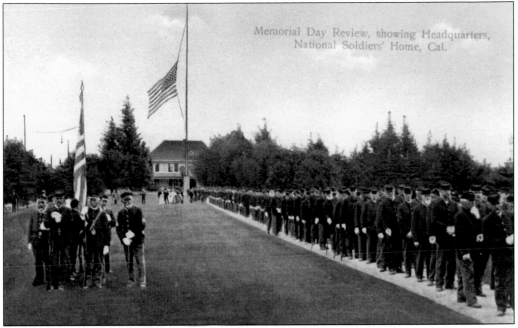

Memorial Day Review, showing Headquarters, National Soldiers' Home, Cal.

SOLDIERS'S HOME REVIEW, EARLY 1900S. Pictured is a Memorial Day review at the National Soldiers Home in West Los Angeles. The headquarters building is visible in the background. In 1887, Senator Jones and Arcadia Bandini de Baker deeded 300 acres near what are now Sawtelle and Wilshire Boulevards to the federal government for the site of a home for disabled military veterans.

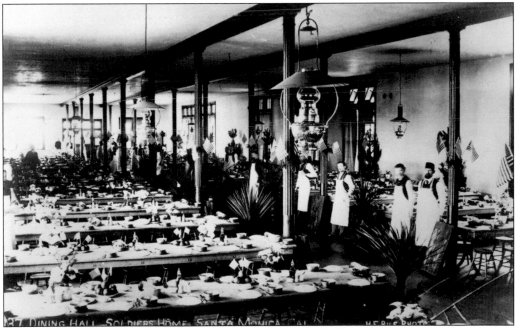

DINING HALL, SOLDIERS'S HOME, EARLY 1900S. In this photograph, the waiters are lined up and ready to serve the veterans. (Courtesy Santa Monica Public Library Image Archives.)

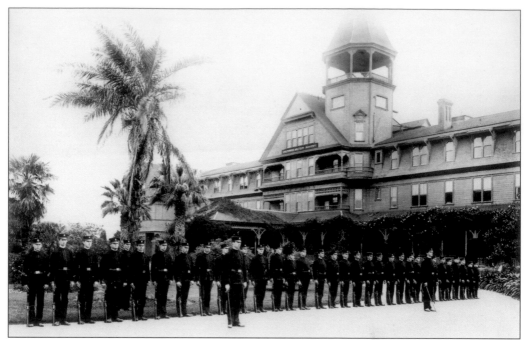

CALIFORNIA MILITARY ACADEMY, EARLY 1900S. This was originally the Arcadia Hotel. It was converted to a military academy and then torn down in 1908. (Santa Monica Historical Society Museum, *Outlook* Collection.)

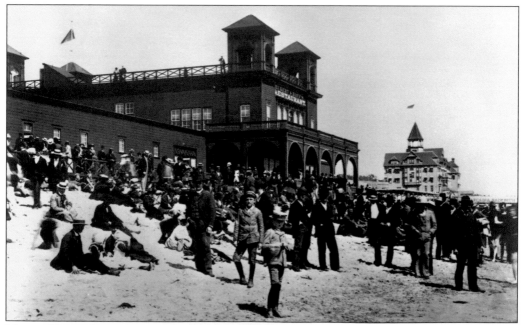

NORTH BEACH BATHHOUSE. The bathhouse, built in 1894, was for many years the area's favorite resort facility. A special feature was the hot saltwater baths. The admission fee was 25¢. The building also housed a restaurant and a bowling pavilion.

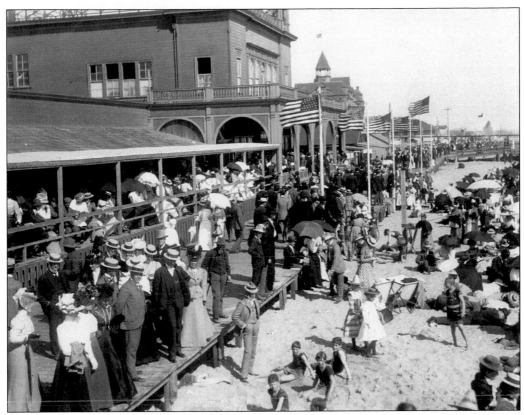

NORTH BEACH BATHHOUSE DRAWS CROWDS, EARLY 1900s. At the beginning of the 20th century, thousands of people were coming to visit the Santa Monica beach and its attractions. In this photograph, crowds of people on the boardwalk in front of the North Beach Bathhouse enjoy a Sunday outing. (Santa Monica Historical Society Museum, Jones Collection.)

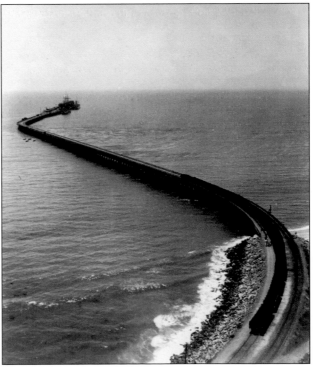

THE LONG WHARF. The Long Wharf was located up the coast from Santa Monica Canyon and served the early Los Angeles shipping industry when it opened in 1893. (Santa Monica Historical Society Museum, *Outlook* Collection.)

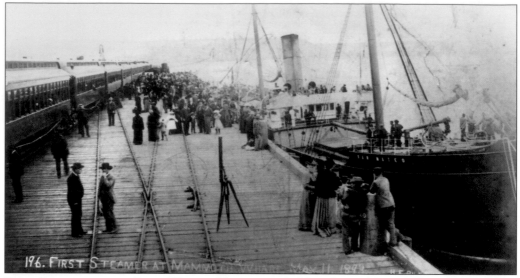

FIRST STEAMER AT THE LONG WHARF. The Long Wharf was located just up the coast from Santa Monica Canyon. When Santa Monica lost the fight to become the area's commercial seaport in 1908, service to the Long Wharf was discontinued and the tracks and facilities were eventually dismantled. (Courtesy Santa Monica Public Library Image Archives.)

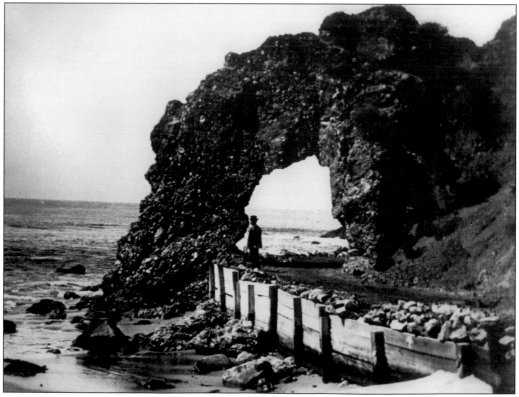

ARCH ROCK, C. 1890. One of Santa Monica's natural wonders, Arch Rock, was so wide that during low tide, horse-drawn wagons could pass through its opening. It was located on what is now Pacific Coast Highway. In 1905, the Arch Rock broke and had to be removed.

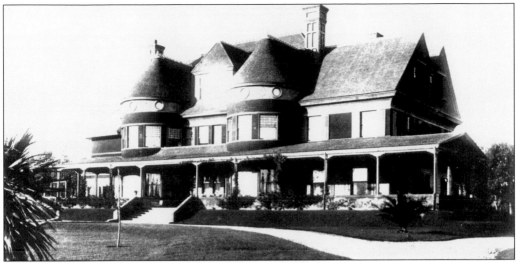

MIRAMAR, FOUNDERS MANSION. Sen. John P. Jones built Miramar, Spanish for "Sea View," in 1889 at a cost of $40,000. The house was built on the corner of Ocean and Nevada (Wilshire) Avenues. The three-story Victorian house had 17 bedrooms, and the gardens contained every kind of fruit and vegetable. Miramar had several owners over the years and was demolished in the 1930s. Today the site houses the Fairmont Miramar Hotel. (Santa Monica Historical Society Museum, Jones Collection.)

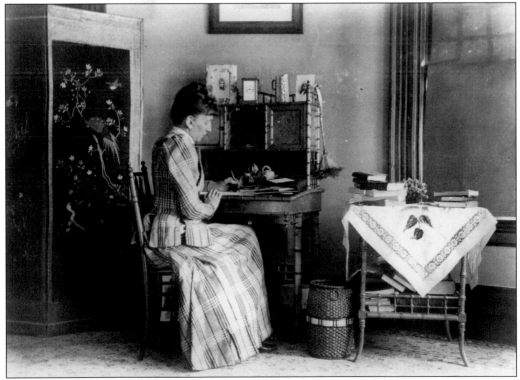

GEORGINA JONES AT HER DESK, LATE 1800S. Georgina Jones spent much time writing to her husband, Senator Jones, who was often away due to his job as a United States senator, a position he held for 30 years. (Santa Monica Historical Society Museum, Jones Collection.)

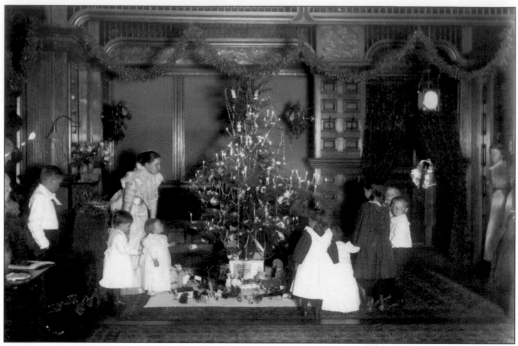

CHRISTMAS AT MIRAMAR, 1897. Celebrating Christmas at Miramar is Senator Jones with his children, grandchildren, young nieces and nephews, and their guests, all gathered around the tree during the holiday get-together. (Santa Monica Historical Society Museum, Jones Collection.)

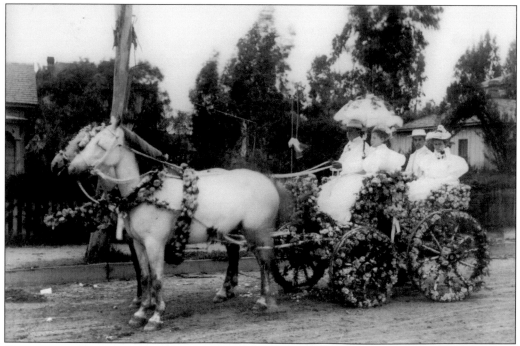

OFF TO THE ROSE PARADE, EARLY 1900s. Jones family members are pictured here in their flower-decorated horse and carriage traveling to the Tournament of Roses Parade in Pasadena. (Santa Monica Historical Society Museum, Jones Collection.)

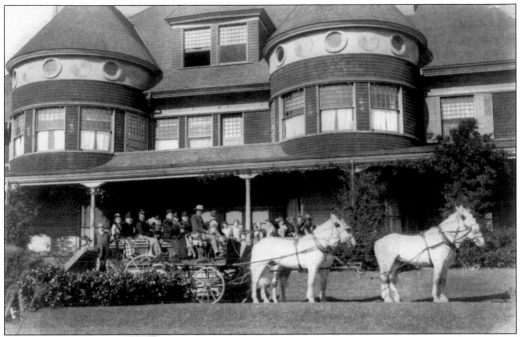

TAKING A RIDE, LATE 1800S. Parked in the front of Senator Jones's mansion are horses and a carriage carrying some of the Jones family members and guests to an outing. (Santa Monica Historical Society Museum, Jones Collection.)

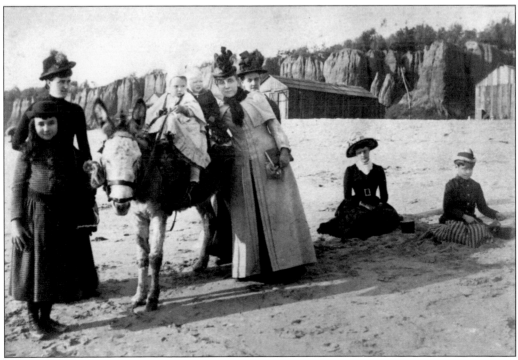

AT THE BEACH. Georgina Jones (center) is pictured here with family members at Santa Monica Beach in the late 1800s. (Santa Monica Historical Society Museum, Jones Collection.)

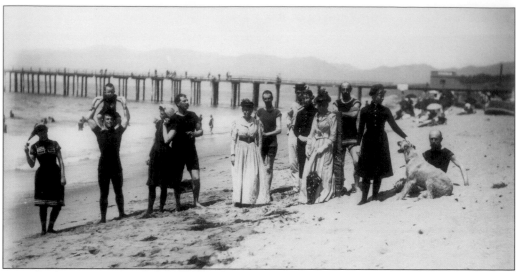

JONES FAMILY ON THE BEACH, EARLY 1900S. Georgina Jones (center), pictured with some of her family members and other relatives, enjoys a day at the beach. (Santa Monica Historical Society Museum, Jones Collection.)

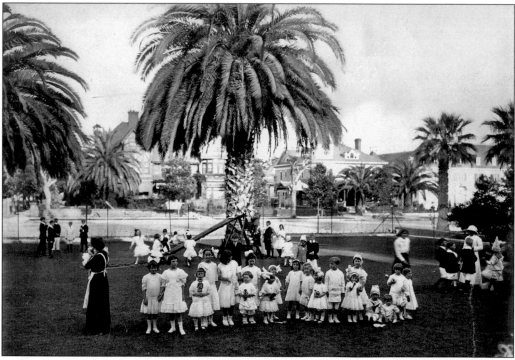

A CHILDREN'S PARTY OUTDOORS AT THE MIRAMAR, EARLY 1900S. According to the late Dorothy Boden, Senator Jones's granddaughter, who lived at Miramar from 1900 to 1906, the house was always full of relatives and their children as well as her parents, Mr. and Mrs. Roy Jones. Roy was the senator's son. Parties were held often for the children. Boden said she and her brother, Gregory, swam in the ocean almost daily. She was about five years old. Most of the children learned to swim in the saltwater plunge of her grandfather Jones's North Beach Bath House. (Santa Monica Historical Society Museum, Jones Collection.)

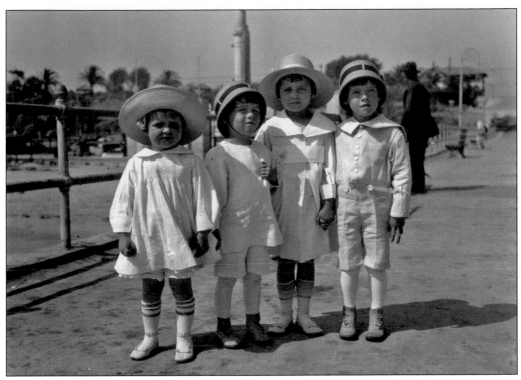

IN THEIR SUNDAY BEST, EARLY 1900S. All dressed up in their Sunday outfits are the grandsons of Senator Jones, Colin and John Farquhar (second and fourth from the left), standing on the early pier with two unidentified children. (Santa Monica Historical Society Museum, Jones Collection.)

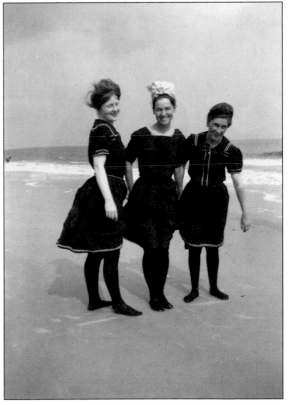

THE JONES SISTERS, LATE 1800S. Alice, Marion, and Georgina Jones, daughters of Santa Monica cofounder John P. Jones, are pictured together at the beach. (Santa Monica Historical Society Museum, Jones Collection.)

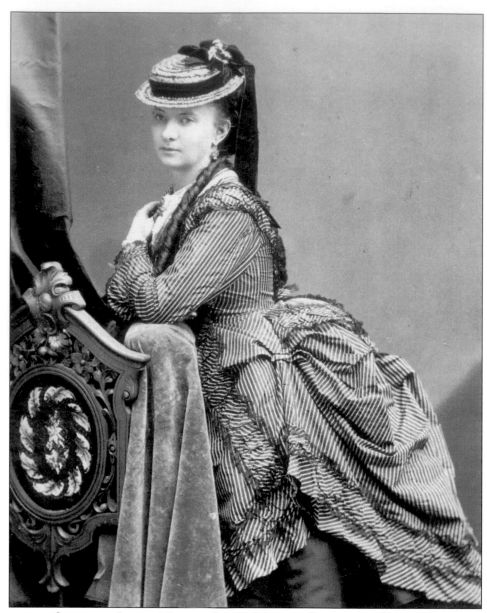

GEORGINA SULLIVAN JONES, WIFE OF SANTA MONICA COFOUNDER JOHN P. JONES, AS A YOUNG WOMAN. Even in her younger days, Georgina wore elegant clothes. After she married Senator Jones, the two of them traveled to Europe where she bought the latest fashions and wore them becomingly. Her hair was always neatly styled. Georgina and the senator had three daughters: Alice, the wife of sculptor and painter Frederick MacMonnies, whose name was well known on all continents; Marion, who married Robert D. Farquhar, a distinguished architect; and Georgina, married to attorney Robert Walton. Georgina and the senator enjoyed traveling to New York, where she lived after her husband's death. While her husband was away in the Senate for 30 years, they wrote often to each other. The collection of letters and other items received by the senator from statesmen, presidents, General Grant, and numerous other notables are being preserved at the Santa Monica Historical Society Museum. (Santa Monica Historical Society Museum, Jones Collection.)

Two

A CITY DEVELOPS

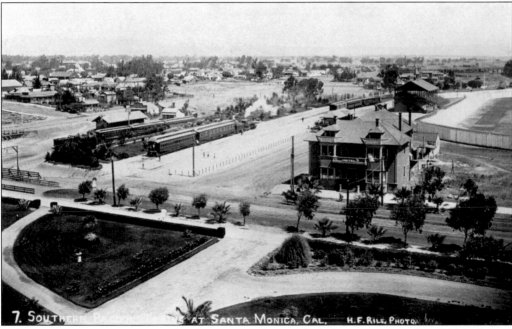

SOUTHERN PACIFIC, C. 1890. This location is where today's Sears store stands at Colorado and Fourth Street. In 1887, a huge influx of people came to California by train and settled in different towns in California, including Santa Monica. By the 1920s, the town had grown into a city. It incorporated in 1886. A board of five trustees, the first officials, were elected and charged with running the city. They soon set laws to govern the city and to improve life in the community. In 1906, the town was governed by seven city council members and a mayor. In 1946, Santa Monicans voted in a council manager form of government. (Santa Monica Historical Society Museum, *Outlook* Collection.)

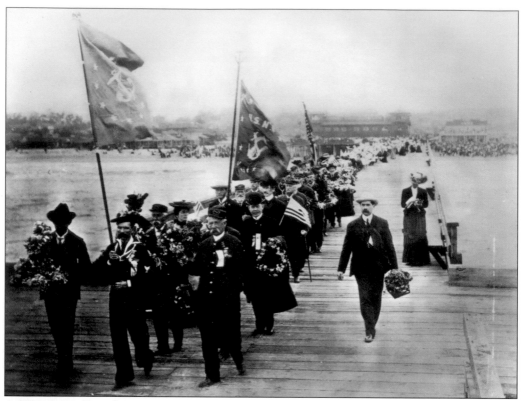

A **MEMORIAL DAY OBSERVANCE ON OCEAN PARK PIER, C. 1900.** The citizens of the town are displaying their patriotism here as they parade on the pier carrying flags and flowers in observance of Memorial Day. (Courtesy Los Angeles Public Library, Security Pacific Bank Collection.)

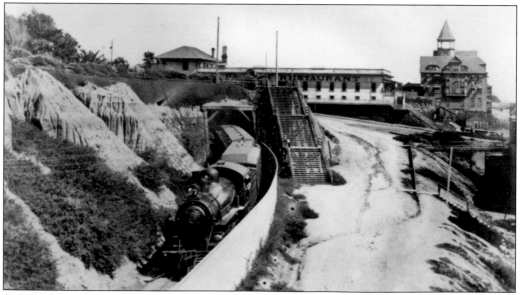

SOUTHERN PACIFIC TRAIN, C. 1800S. A Southern Pacific train emerges from the tunnel under Ocean Avenue on its way to the Long Wharf. These tracks were later replaced by a dirt road called Roosevelt Highway, and the tunnel was eventually enlarged for today's Pacific Coast Highway.

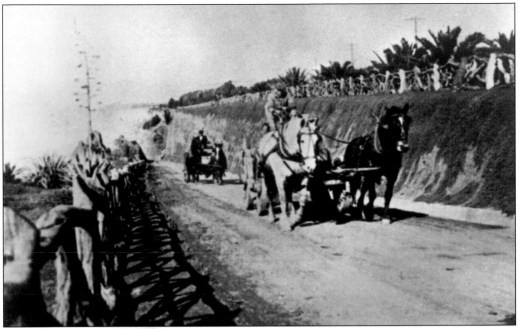

CALIFORNIA INCLINE. Horse-drawn wagons were able to haul freight up the California Incline, pictured here in 1915, after the cliffs were scaled back to make way for the construction of a dirt road.

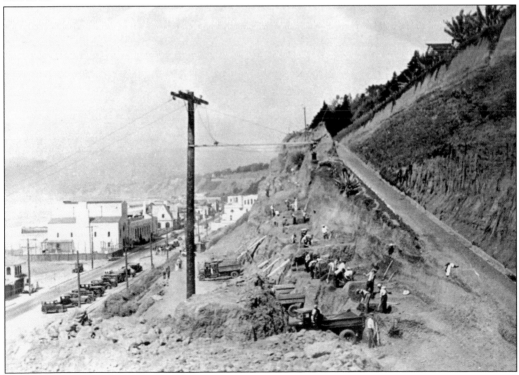

CALIFORNIA INCLINE, C. 1920S. Men work at widening the California Incline in Santa Monica. The incline linked Ocean Avenue to Pacific Coast Highway. (Courtesy Marshall Hickson.)

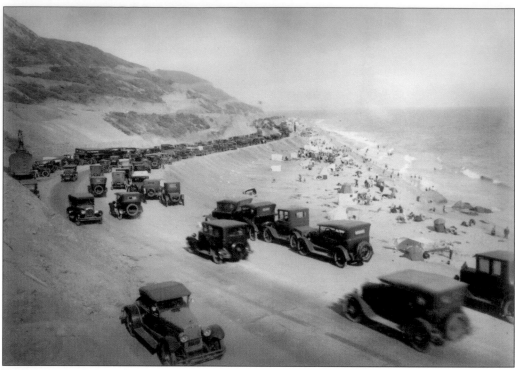

Traffic along the Beach, c. 1927. The beaches and highway were just as crowded in the early days as they are today. The Pacific Coast Highway was not yet fully developed.

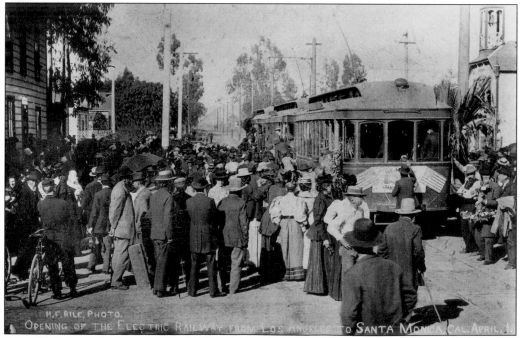

First Electric Streetcar, 1896. Residents of Santa Monica gathered to welcome the city's first electric streetcar, which began service from Los Angeles to their beach community. (Santa Monica Historical Society Museum, *Outlook* Collection.)

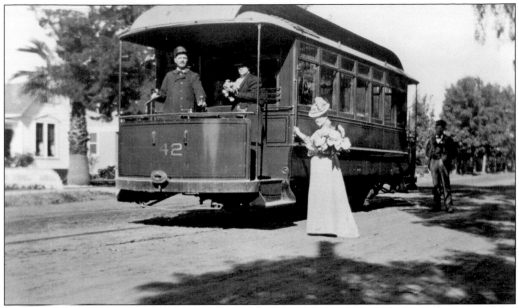

A TROLLEY STOP. The Los Angeles Pacific trolley line makes a stop in Santa Monica around the early 1900s. (Santa Monica Historical Society Museum, *Outlook* Collection.)

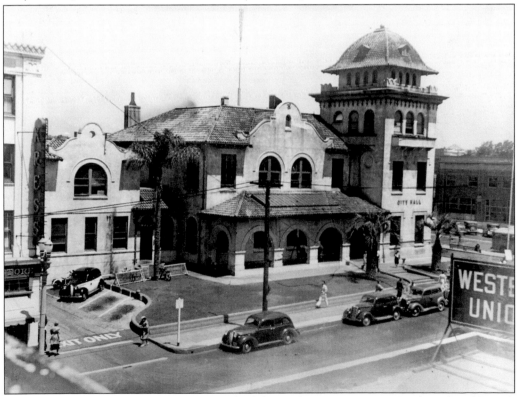

SANTA MONICA CITY HALL. The old city hall, located at Santa Monica Boulevard and Fourth Street, served the city from 1902 to 1938. It also housed the police department. Today's city hall, located at 1685 Main Street, replaced this earlier structure in 1939.

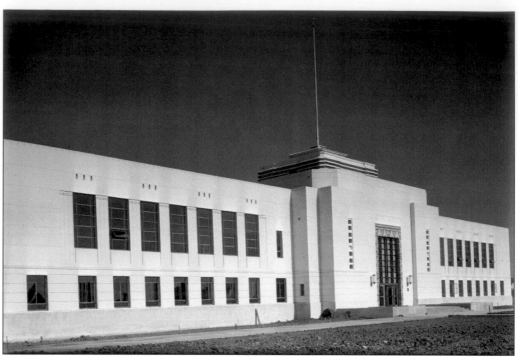

SANTA MONICA CITY HALL. This photograph shows city hall nearing completion in 1939 at Main Street near Colorado Avenue. The cost for the site and building was $350,000. (Santa Monica Historical Society Museum, Beebe Collection.)

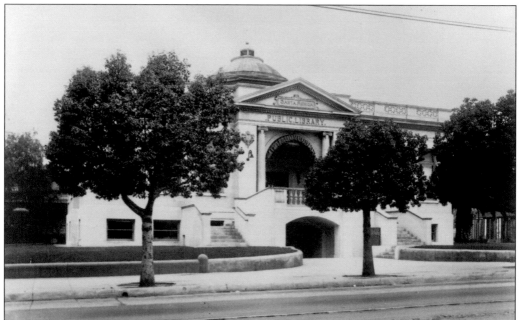

SANTA MONICA LIBRARY. Andrew Carnegie pledged a gift of $12,500 to Santa Monica for a new library building, provided the city furnish the land as well as a "free public" library. A site was found on the northeast corner of Oregon (Santa Monica Boulevard) Avenue and Fifth Street. The structure was dedicated on August 11, 1904.

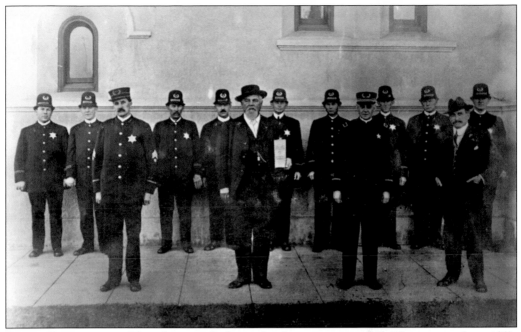

POLICE DEPARTMENT. This photograph shows the department in 1909. The man in the middle is Juan J. Carrillo, the first judge, mayor, and city trustee of Santa Monica for many years. He did much in the early days to lay the foundation upon which the city of today was developed. (Courtesy Richard Tapia.)

POLICE CHIEF CLARENCE WEBB. In 1916, Webb entered the police department as a clerk. He held practically every position in the police department and was the first appointed chief in 1924. Under Chief Webb, the department was raised to a high state of efficiency; the equipment of the department ranked with the best of any city of comparable size. At that time, the department had a fleet of nine automobiles and five motorcycles. (Courtesy Los Angeles Public Library, Security Pacific Bank Collection.)

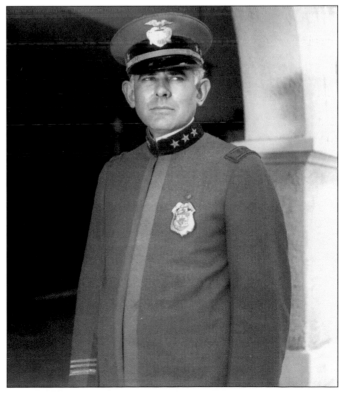

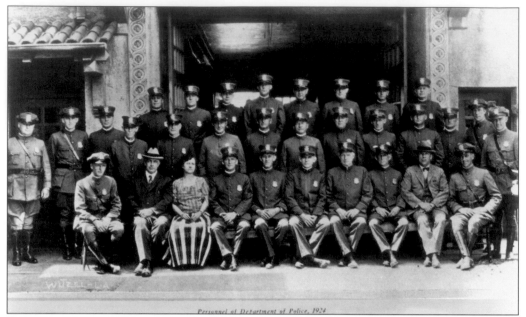

PERSONNEL OF THE DEPARTMENT OF POLICE, SANTA MONICA, 1924. It was in May 1897 that the police department was created. Messrs. George F. See and A. L. Forsyth were appointed policemen. In 1897, Max Barretto left his position at Port Los Angeles to become Santa Monica's first chief of police. For much of the early years, the police devoted their time to rounding up drunks, primarily those staggering out of saloons. Lacking a paddy wagon, the method of transport to the lockup was a wheelbarrow. (Courtesy Richard Tapia.)

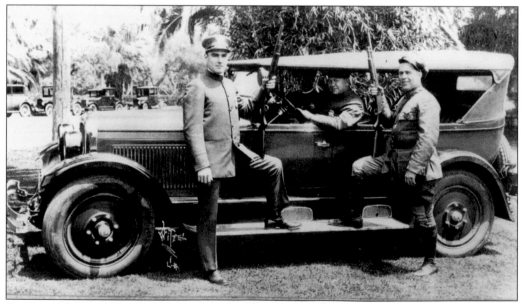

SHOTGUN SQUAD. The Santa Monica Police Department Shotgun Squad, pictured here in 1927, are A. G. Osten; William O. Bray, motorcycle sergeant; W. P. Myatt, driver; and William Blackett. (Courtesy Richard Tapia.)

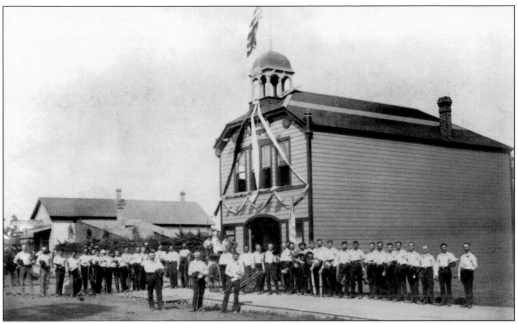

SANTA MONICA FIRE DEPARTMENT, C. 1910. The department was located at Fourth Street and Oregon (Santa Monica Boulevard) Avenue. The men who belonged to the first fire department received no pay. In 1906, the town's board of trustees purchased a hose wagon, a chemical engine, and a team of horses, and hired a driver. As the town grew, the fire department improved. The volunteer system was abandoned in 1916, and the department now hired its firemen. (Santa Monica Historical Society Museum, *Outlook* Collection.)

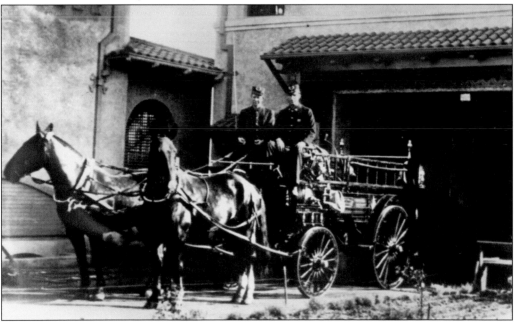

FIRE COMPANY NO. 1, EARLY 1900s. The fire department, located at Fourth Street and Oregon (Santa Monica Boulevard) Avenue behind city hall, is seen in this 1910 photograph. The horse-drawn hose cart was later replaced by motorized fire equipment in 1913.

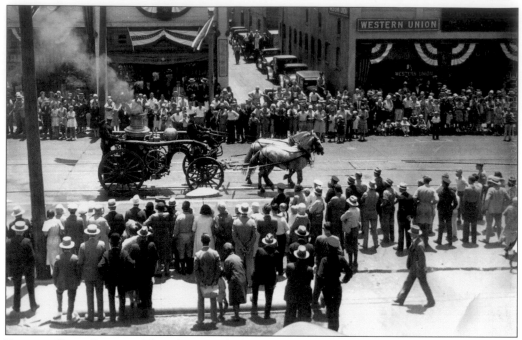

PIONEER DAYS PARADE. This photograph shows a Los Angeles Fire Department steam engine in the 1940 Santa Monica Pioneers Day parade. The annual parade drew thousands of people. (Santa Monica Historical Society Museum, *Outlook* Collection.)

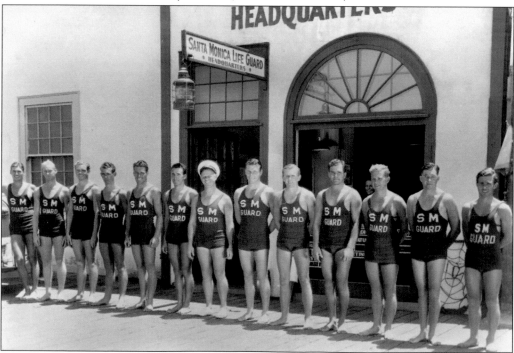

SANTA MONICA LIFEGUARDS, 1932. Capt. George Watkins (wearing the white hat) was head of the lifeguards, who are lined up here in front of their headquarters that was located for a short time in the La Monica Ballroom on the Santa Monica Pier.

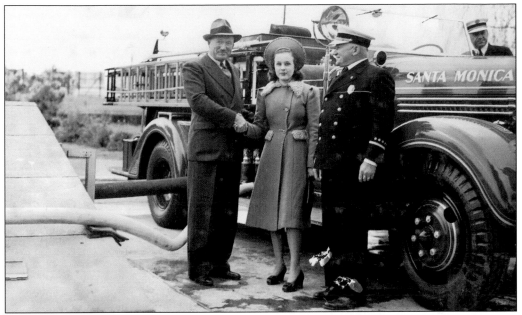

ACTRESS DEANNA DURBIN, C. 1939. Durbin is pictured here with police chief Charles Dice and fire chief William Mohr beside a Santa Monica fire truck.

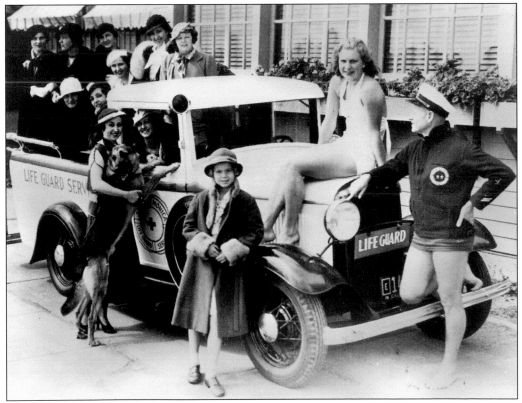

LIFEGUARD SERVICE AUTOMOBILE, C. 1935. In this photograph is lifeguard captain George Watkins (right) with a group of ladies eager to learn about the lifeguard service.

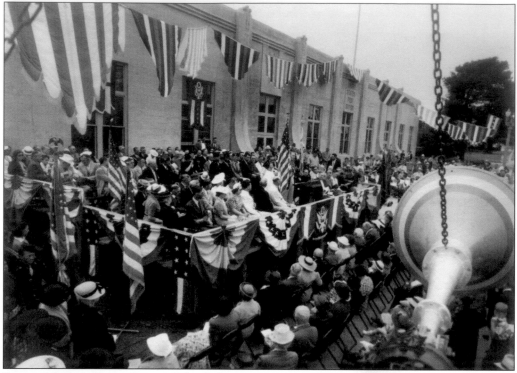

Santa Monica Post Office. The dedication ceremony for the new main post office at Fifth Street and Arizona Avenue took place on July 24, 1938. The post office paid $46,000 for the site. It was designed in the Moderne style by architect Robert Dennis Murray. (Courtesy Santa Monica Post Office.)

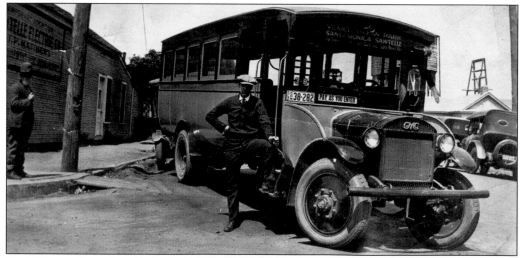

Bay Cities Bus. Bay Cities bought four Dodge buses in 1922 to begin service on Wilshire Boulevard. The 20-foot ebony buses sported red pin-striping and allowed from 25 to 30 passengers on the perimeter bench seats. The first blue and white bus began service along Pico Boulevard on April 14, 1928. A 15¢ fare was charged for those wishing to ride from end to end. Local rides cost 5¢. During the first week, a total of 16,000 passengers flocked to the new bus route. (Courtesy Big Blue Bus.)

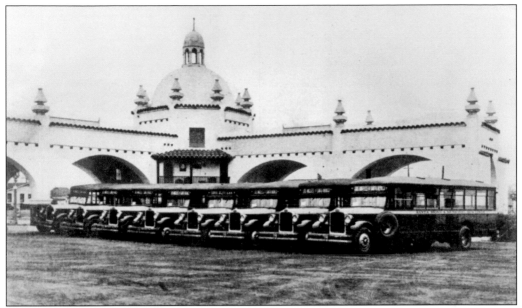

BIG BLUE BUS. The first Big Blue Bus facility was a gas station known as Hendrick's Corner, located at the intersection of Pico and Lincoln Boulevards. Pictured here are the city's first eight buses purchased in July 1928. (Courtesy Big Blue Bus.)

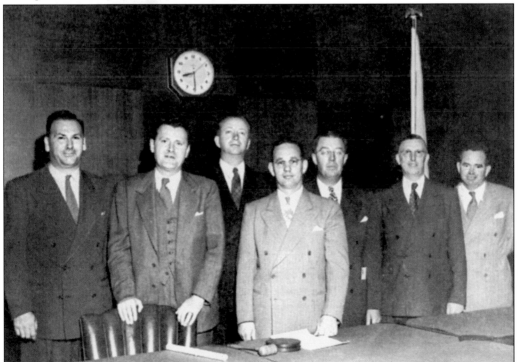

THE CITY COUNCIL OF SANTA MONICA. First to hold the office since the adoption of the council-manager form of government in 1946, from left to right, are Jack Guercio, H. G. Markworth, Ben Bernard, Mayor Mark T. Gates, J. L. Schimmer Jr., George Neilson, and Edwin L. Talmadge. (Courtesy City of Santa Monica.)

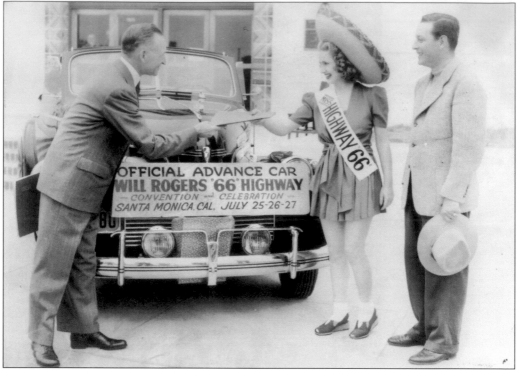

HIGHWAY 66 CONVENTION. Mayor Samuel Crawford is pictured here with Miss Highway 66 and an unidentified man at the Will Rogers 66 Highway Convention and Celebration. This could be in conjunction with a plaque dedicated to humorist Will Rogers in 1952, naming Highway 66 as the Will Rogers Highway. The plaque is located in Palisades Park at the foot of Santa Monica Boulevard. (Courtesy Ted Fach.)

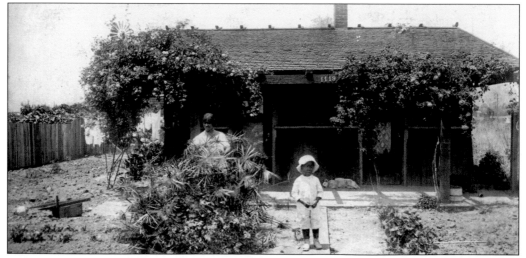

HOUSE ON MAIN STREET. In the early 1900s, this house was built on Main Street in Ocean Park. In 1926, Main Street was widened on its west side, and several existing buildings were moved back four feet from the previous property line. From this date until the beginning of the Depression, several significant buildings were constructed on the street. Today Main Street is a thriving business area.

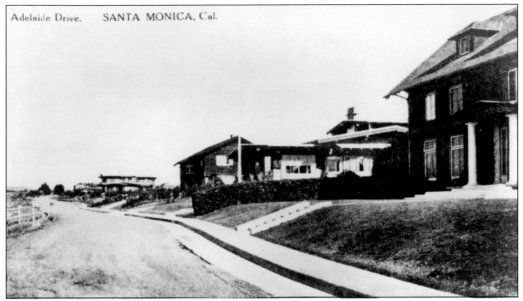

ADELAIDE DRIVE. On the rim of Santa Monica Canyon is Adelaide Drive. Since the opening of the tract in 1905 and annexation to the city in 1906, Adelaide Drive has attracted numerous prominent Southern Californians who hired the best architects to create summer, and later year-round, homes for them.

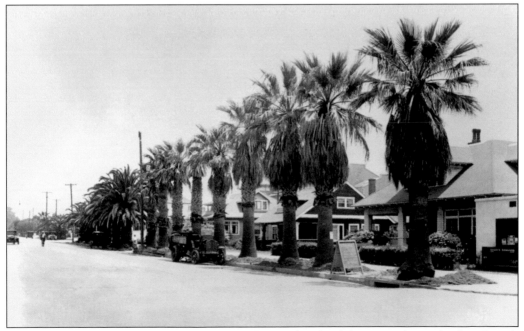

WILSHIRE BOULEVARD, 1920S. This shows the south side of the street from Third to Fourth Street. These homes were later replaced with businesses.

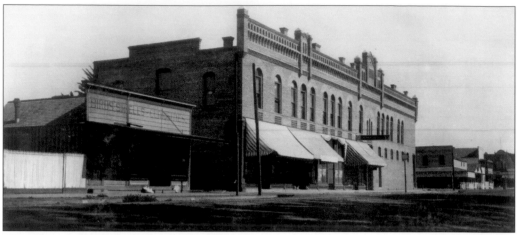

WHITWORTH BUILDING LOCATED ON BROADWAY, A DIRT ROAD IN THE LATE 1800s. Shortly after incorporation in November 1886, the first board of trustees began to improve the town. Taxes were high, but the citizens were willing to pay. They knew the town must be improved. Within a few years, the dusty streets were graded and spread with gravel. A sprinkling wagon went up and down the streets in summer to keep down the dust. Sidewalks were also put in. (Santa Monica Historical Society Museum, Jones Collection.)

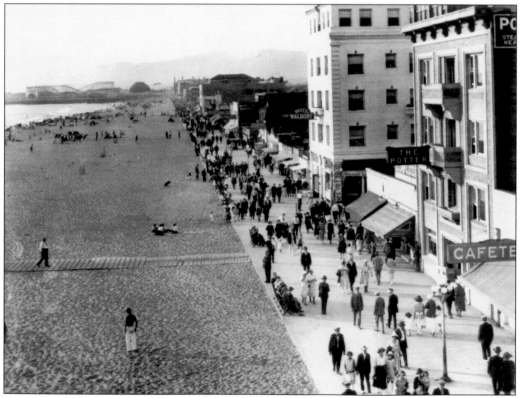

OCEANFRONT WALK LOOKING NORTH FROM THE VENICE PLUNGE TOWER, 1922. This view is looking north from the Venice Plunge Tower. It was a convenient walkway between the Ocean Park Piers and the Santa Monica Pier. There was always a lot of foot traffic on this convenient and popular route.

Three

EVERYDAY LIFE
SCHOOLS, CHURCHES, AND EVENTS

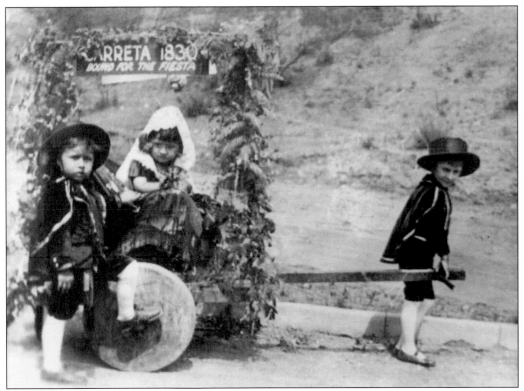

CHILDREN'S PARADE, C. 1929. Riding in the Children's Parade in Ocean Park are Rosemary Miano (center), Vincent Romero (left), and Perfecto Marquez (right), all descendants of Francisco Marquez I and Ysidro Reyes I, grantees of Rancho Boca de Santa Monica in 1839. The *carretta*, or carriage, was made by Ysidro Reyes II out of sycamore trees, and he even made the nails, called pegs, out of sycamore wood. In 1886, three little churches were dedicated in the town—the Methodist, the Presbyterian, and Episcopal. A three-room school was completed. For entertainment, there were parades and bathing-beauty contests. (Courtesy Rosemary Miano.)

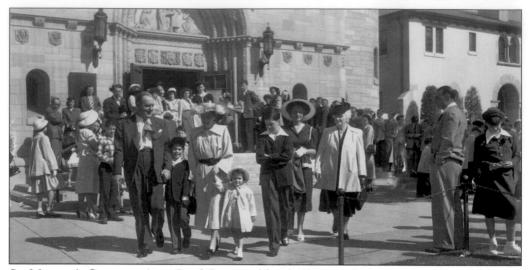

ST. MONICA'S CHURCH. Actor Pat O'Brien and family (front row), along with other parishioners, gather outside of St. Monica's Church following the Easter Sunday service on April 7, 1949. The church, school, high school, rectory, and convent occupy the block from California Avenue to Washington Avenue between Seventh Street and Lincoln Boulevard, having been moved to this location from the original 1884 site at Third Street and Santa Monica Boulevard. The church was completed in 1925 under the leadership of Monsignor Nicholas Conneally, rector from 1923 to 1949. The statue on the northeast corner of Seventh Street and California Avenue is dedicated to Monsignor Conneally. (Santa Monica Historical Society Museum, Beebe Collection.)

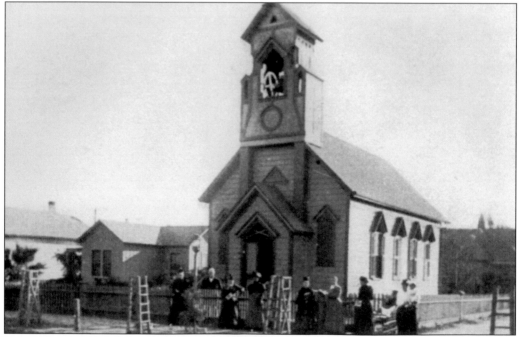

FIRST CHURCH OF SANTA MONICA. Pictured here is the early Methodist Episcopal Church, founded on October 15, 1875. It was located at Sixth Street and Arizona Avenue and erected on two lots. The value of the lots, building, and grounds was about $1,500. (Santa Monica Historical Society Museum, *Outlook* Collection.)

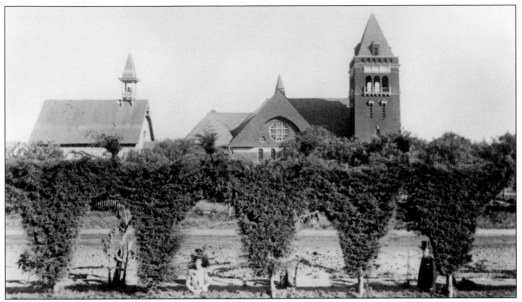

PRESBYTERIAN CHURCH. The original Presbyterian church in Santa Monica was erected in 1886 on property at Third Street and Arizona Avenue, donated by Sen. John P. Jones and Col. Robert S. Baker, cofounders of Santa Monica. The church cost about $7,000 to build. Both the Methodist and Presbyterian churches claim to be the first church in Santa Monica. (Santa Monica Historical Society Museum, *Outlook* Collection.)

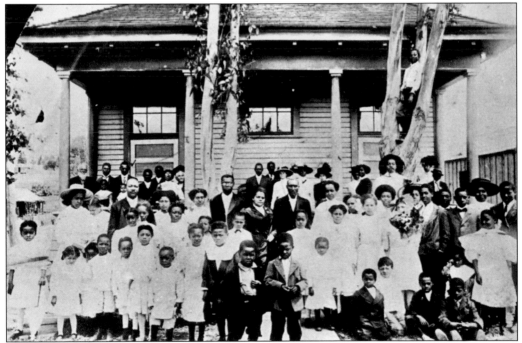

PHILLIPS CHAPEL C.M.E. CHURCH, 1910. Phillips Chapel at Fourth and Bay Streets was founded by Bishop Charles Henry Phillips. It is the oldest Christian Methodist Episcopal Church on the Pacific Coast and the oldest African American church in Santa Monica. (Courtesy Santa Monica Public Library Image Archives/Donald A. Brunson Sr. Collection.)

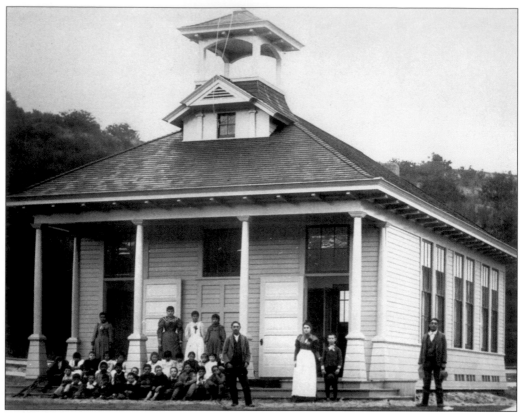

Santa Monica Canyon School. Children from surrounding farms and ranches attended the one-room school in the canyon, pictured here in 1894. Today the building serves as a library for the Canyon Elementary School. It is the oldest school structure in Los Angeles still in use. (Courtesy Angie Marquez Olivera.)

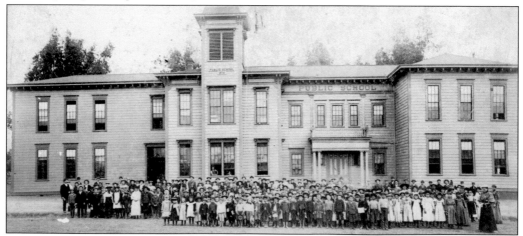

Santa Monica's First School, Sixth Street School. Within four months after the first lots were sold in Santa Monica in 1875, the population had reached 600. Citizens of the new town levied a tax for school purposes, and a public school opened in March 1876. At the one-teacher school, 66 boys and girls crowded into a small classroom. This photograph shows the school after several additions were made. (Courtesy Santa Monica Public Library Image Archives.)

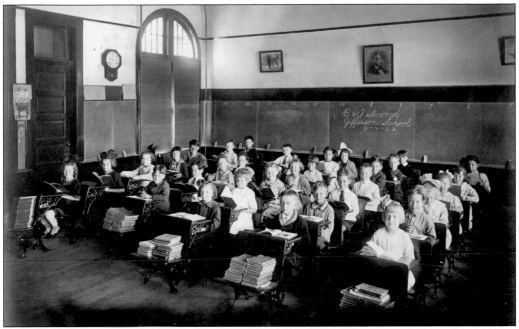

JEFFERSON SCHOOL CLASSROOM. A bond issue in 1906 provided funds for the construction of three additional schools in Santa Monica, the first of which was to replace the old Sixth Street School and named Jefferson School.

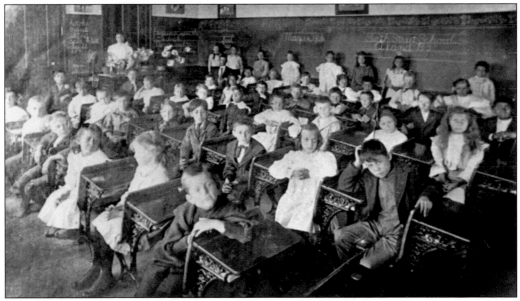

SIXTH STREET SCHOOL CLASSROOM IN 1906. In those days, teachers were allowed to use corporal punishment on a child. This ad was placed in a newspaper in the late 1800s, "Wanted, a district school teacher. The board of directors of the Santa Monica School District are authorized to have a teacher for the summer session which commences July 12 in Steeres Opera House. He must be a man, sound in body and intellect and not afraid to use the rod. Wages $10.00 per month and board found." On March 10, 1893, the board of trustees by resolution decreed that teachers in the public schools of the town were forbidden to use corporal punishment upon any pupil.

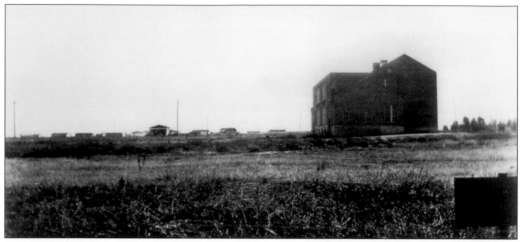

FRANKLIN SCHOOL. The school, located at Twenty-fifth Street and Montana Avenue, opened in 1925. It was a two-story brick building with seven classrooms that included kindergarten through fourth grade. There was no fence around the playground, which was dirt or mud depending on the weather. The school was out in the country and very few homes were around. (Courtesy Donald Howland.)

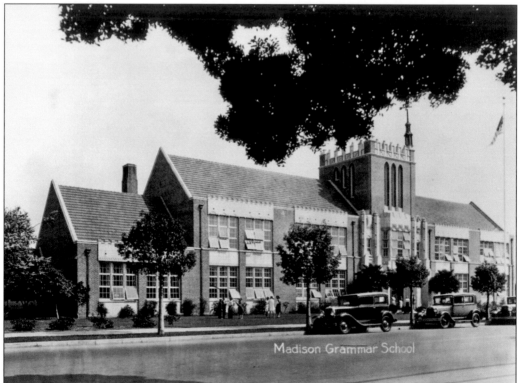

MADISON SCHOOL. This is the second-oldest school site in Santa Monica. The block was the location of the city's first separate high school in 1897, originally known as Lincoln School. Madison Elementary School, a two-story building, was constructed in 1926 with Francis David Rutherford as the architect. Like all Santa Monica schools, it was closed following the 1933 earthquake and tents were used until its reopening in 1938. (Courtesy Santa Monica School District.)

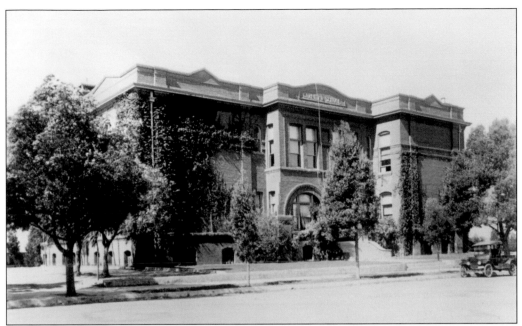

GARFIELD SCHOOL. In 1913, Garfield School had the distinction of starting the first kindergarten in Santa Monica. It was a necessity because of the large number of working mothers with small children. Another "first" at Garfield was the establishment of the Parent-Teacher Association. (Courtesy Santa Monica School District.)

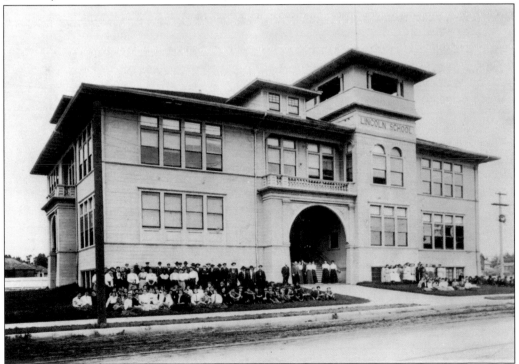

LINCOLN SCHOOL. This first Lincoln School opened in 1898 at Tenth Street and Santa Monica Boulevard and served as a high school. (Courtesy Santa Monica School District.)

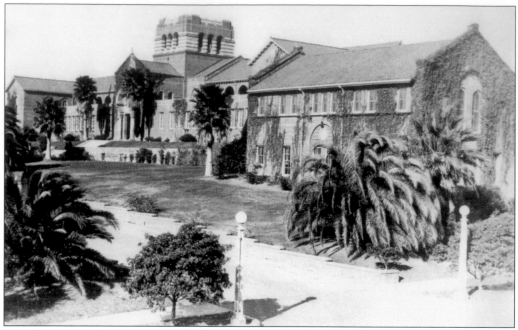

SANTA MONICA HIGH SCHOOL. The school, built in 1912 on what was called Prospect Hill, was dedicated on February 13, 1913. In 1912, a contest was held to name the new school paper. A boy who lived in the canyon won with the name "Samohi," which he derived by using the first two letters in each of the following words: Santa Monica High. The name was soon applied to the school. (Courtesy Santa Monica School District.)

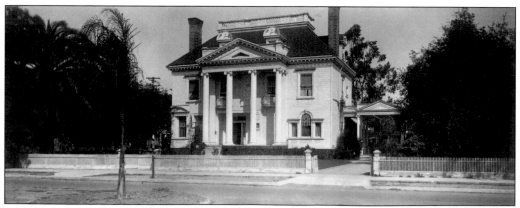

ACADEMY OF HOLY NAMES. A band of Sisters of the Holy Names established the Academy of Holy Names in 1901, for many years a flourishing school for girls. It was located at Third Street and Arizona Avenue.

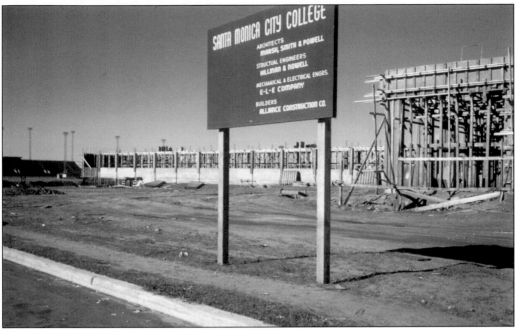

SANTA MONICA CITY COLLEGE. This photograph shows the Santa Monica City College under construction. The college was established as a junior college in 1929. It was originally housed in a few upstairs rooms of the early Lincoln High School at Seventh Street and Michigan avenue. The new building was completed in February 1952. (Courtesy Herb Roney.)

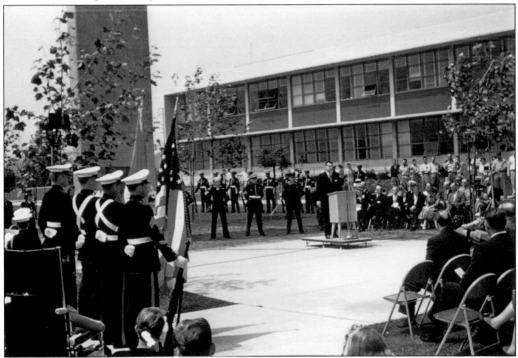

SANTA MONICA CITY COLLEGE DEDICATION, 1952. Now called Santa Monica College, it is located at 1900 Pico Boulevard. (Courtesy Herb Roney.)

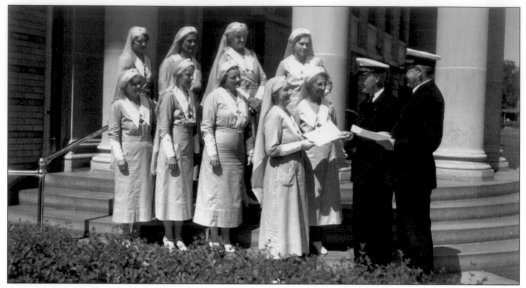

RED CROSS OF SANTA MONICA. Pictured here are Red Cross Gray Ladies receiving certificates on September 18, 1936. The first year a disaster-relief committee formed was in 1920. In 1921, the disaster team responded to the "great fire" in Venice, and victims were given room and board at the Sawtelle Soldiers Home. Chapter volunteers continue to help victims of fires, earthquakes, and floods locally, nationally, and internationally. (Santa Monica Historical Society Museum, Bill Beebe Collection.)

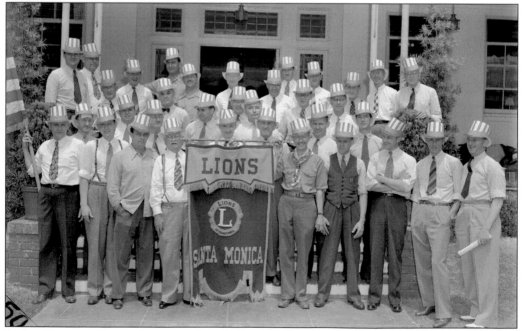

LIONS CLUB OF SANTA MONICA. "Uncle Sam at Work" was the theme chosen by the Lions Club for club members operating the victory house with the avowed intention of breaking all previous records in the sale of war bonds and stamps. The club set a goal of raising $200,000. This photograph was taken July 9, 1942. (Santa Monica Historical Society Museum, Bill Beebe Collection.)

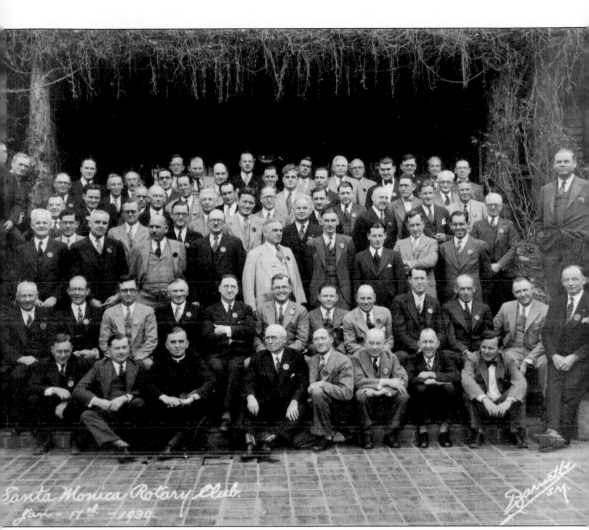

SANTA MONICA ROTARY CLUB, 1930. On February 11, 1922, the club was officially chartered as club member 1086. The Rotary Club donates funds to worthy local charities and organizations. Paul P. Harris was the founder of Rotary in 1868, which was the world's first and most international service club. Rotary is an organization of business and professional leaders united worldwide who provide humanitarian service, promote high ethical standards in all vocations, and help build goodwill and peace in the world. The idea of a Rotary Club in Santa Monica originated with four businessmen in 1920. Ernest English took the lead in organizing the club. (Courtesy Roma Rutherford Cockins.)

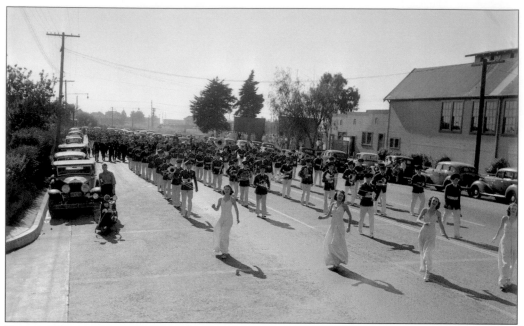

KIWANIS PARADE, 1938. Everyone loves a parade, and the one pictured here was held by the Kiwanis Club. Founded in 1922, Kiwanis is a global organization of volunteers dedicated to changing the world for the better, one child and one community at a time. (Santa Monica Historical Society Museum, Bill Beebe Collection.)

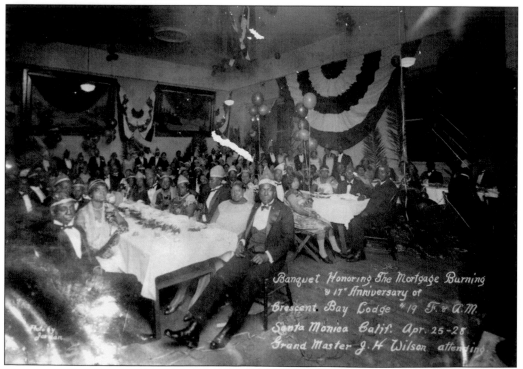

CRESCENT BAY LODGE NO. 19. This banquet is honoring the mortgage burning and 17th anniversary of the lodge on April 25, 1925. (Courtesy Crescent Bay Lodge No. 19.)

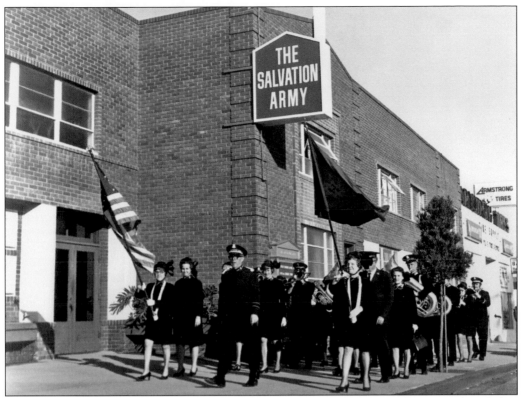

SALVATION ARMY OFFICERS PARADE. The Salvation Army Santa Monica Corps was founded in July 1893. During World War II, services expanded to include a USO for the armed forces. Kettle Day in Santa Monica started in 1891. The Women's Auxiliary was founded in 1964 to assist with the Salvation Army's programs for the needy. (Courtesy Salvation Army.)

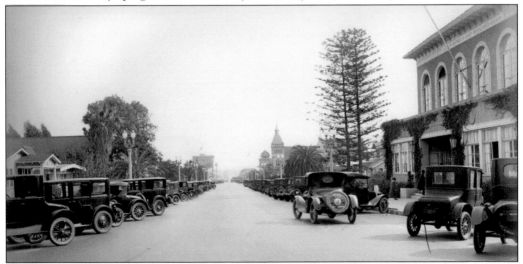

FOURTH STREET, C. 1930. This view is looking south from Wilshire Boulevard. On the right is the landmark Santa Monica Bay Woman's Club, a philanthropic organization, which was founded in 1905. Arcadia Bandini de Baker donated funds for the land on which the club building was constructed in 1914. (Santa Monica Historical Society Museum, Bill Beebe Collection.)

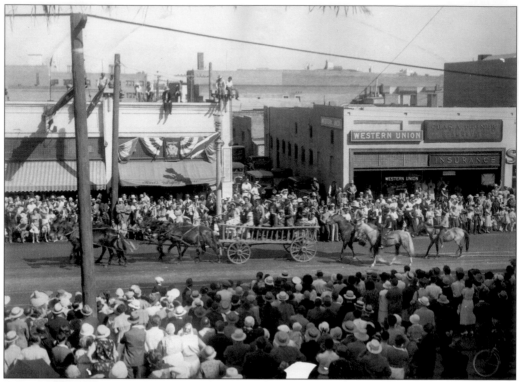

PIONEER DAY PARADE, C. 1930. Frank Hauser, who operated the Pioneer Market on Third Street, originated the Pioneer Day celebration in Santa Monica to celebrate his father's crossing of the plains in a covered wagon. The event became so popular that more merchants and businesses joined in. By 1936, the parade drew 225,000 people. Participants in the parade included mayors, governors, movie stars, and other notables.

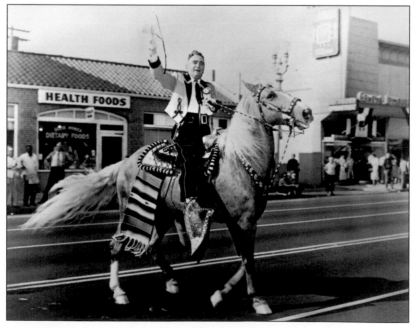

SHERIFF EUGENE BISCAILUZ. The sheriff is pictured here riding in the Pioneer Day parade in Santa Monica in the 1930s. He was sheriff of Los Angeles County for over 25 years and lived in Santa Monica for over 20 years.

Four

PLEASURE PIERS

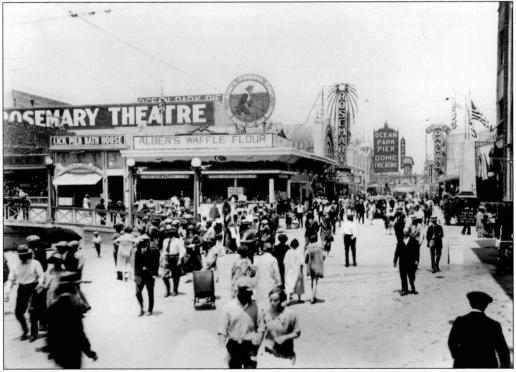

A WEEKEND CROWD AT THE OCEAN PARK PIER. Some of the early piers in Ocean Park were the Horseshoe Pier and Pavilion, Crystal Pier, and the Million Dollar Pier, which replaced the old Horseshoe Pier in 1911 but was destroyed by fire two years later. At the same location, three side-by-side piers were built—the Pickering Pleasure Pier, the G. M. Jones Pier, and the Dome Pier. Ocean Park was at its heyday during the early 1900s. Pleasure seekers were lured to the piers with exciting rides, casinos, dance halls, plunges, theaters, and saloons. In 1924, most of Ocean Park's amusement piers were destroyed by fire. During that year, the La Monica Ballroom's gala opening on Santa Monica Pier was attended by 25,000 people, including many of Hollywood's most famous silent film stars. (Courtesy Ed Tynan.)

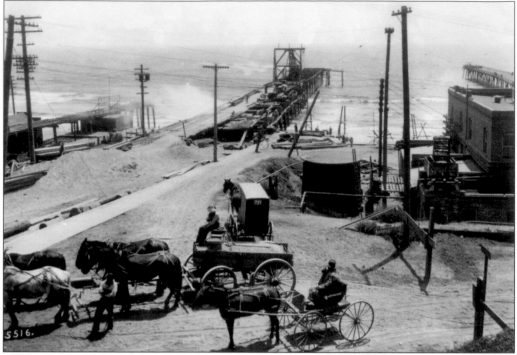

SANTA MONICA PIER BEING BUILT. Construction started on the concrete Santa Monica Municipal Pier in May 1908. It was located at the foot of Colorado Avenue between the stub of the old railroad wharf and the North Beach Pier. (Santa Monica Historical Society Museum, *Outlook* Collection.)

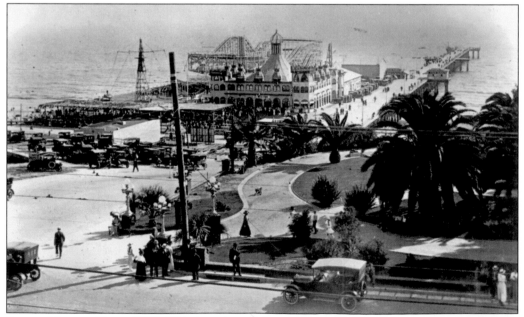

SANTA MONICA PIER, 1920. This is a view of the pier from Ocean Avenue and Palisades Park. The domed carousel building is pictured in the center of the photograph. Charles Looff built the pier. (Courtesy Jane Newcomb Whiting.)

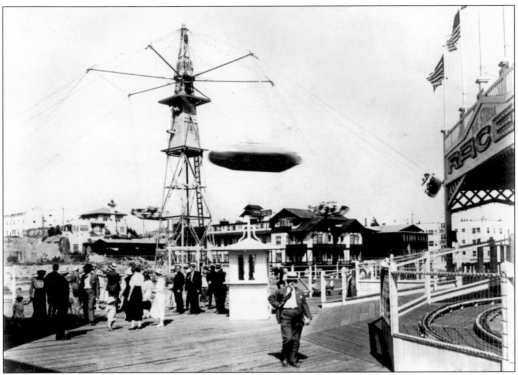

SANTA MONICA PIER, C. 1920S. This photograph shows one of the rides at the pier (center). The Aeroscope whirled passengers around at 35 miles per hour in six-passenger flying boats. (Courtesy Jane Newcomb Whiting.)

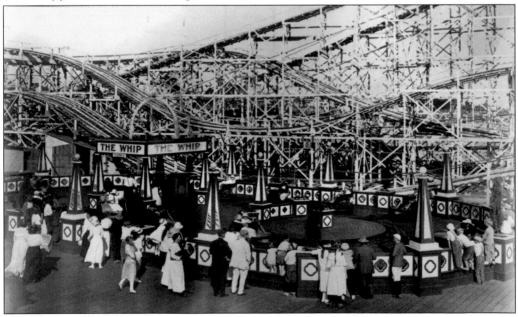

THE WHIP, SANTA MONICA PIER, C. 1920S. In this photograph, parents are watching while their children are whirled about on The Whip, one of the many amusements enjoyed at the Looff Pleasure Pier. (Courtesy Jane Newcomb Whiting.)

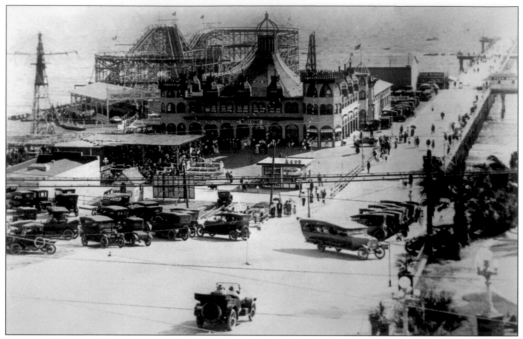

SANTA MONICA PIER, 1920s. The pier is probably the city's most widely recognized landmark. It was originally two different piers. The original 1,600-foot-long municipal pier was dedicated September 9, 1909, before a crowd of over 5,000 people. The Looff Pier, which contained the carousel building, was constructed in 1916 by Charles Looff. This pier was later owned and operated as the Newcomb Pier until the city purchased it in 1974. (Courtesy Jane Newcomb Whiting.)

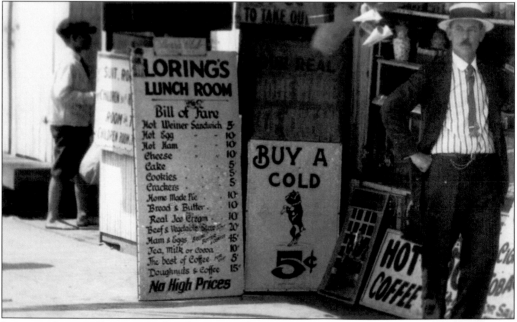

LORINGS LUNCH ROOM. The lunchroom on the Santa Monica Pier advertised "No High Prices" in this 1925 photograph—hot dogs and soda pop cost a nickel each and homemade pies were 10¢. (Santa Monica Historical Society Museum, *Outlook* Collection.)

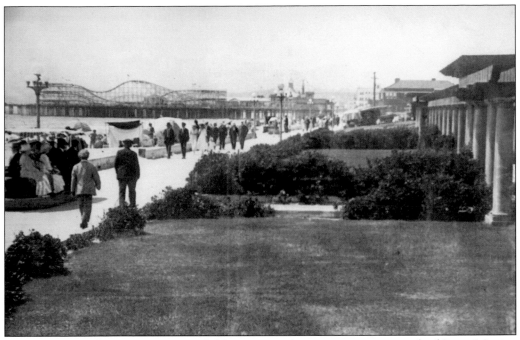

ELECTRIC TRAM SERVICE, C. 1920S. A 20-passenger electric tram service, south of Santa Monica Pier, ran along the Ocean Front Promenade between the Ocean Park and Looff Piers. (Courtesy Jane Newcomb Whiting.)

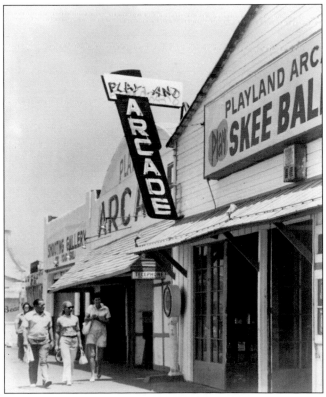

THE ARCADE, SANTA MONICA PIER, C. 1940S. The Playland Arcade, owned by the George Gordon family, is one of the oldest businesses on the pier. (Courtesy George Gordon.)

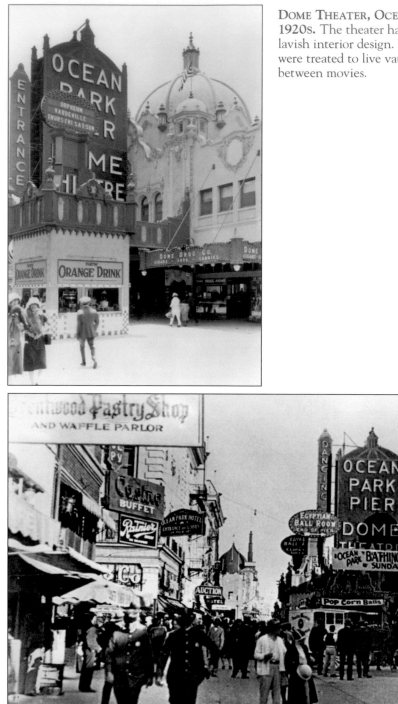

DOME THEATER, OCEAN PARK PIER, 1920S. The theater had 1,600 seats and a lavish interior design. Weekend audiences were treated to live vaudeville acts on stage between movies.

OCEAN PARK PIER, C. 1920S. The pier was Santa Monica's most popular amusement area for many years and drew hundreds of thousands of visitors. (Santa Monica Historical Society Museum, *Outlook* Collection.)

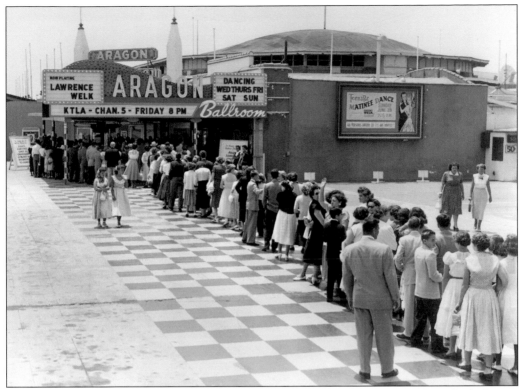

ARAGON BALLROOM, C. 1940S. Lawrence Welk and his band drew huge crowds to the ballroom at the Ocean Park Pier. Dodge dealers of Southern California became sponsors of the Welk show because of its popularity. It eventually became a favorite show on national television. (Santa Monica Historical Society Museum, Bill Beebe Collection.)

CASINO GARDENS, 1940S. Harry James, Benny Goodman, and their bands played swing music at the Casino Gardens on the Ocean Park Pier. (Santa Monica Historical Society Museum, Bill Beebe Collection.)

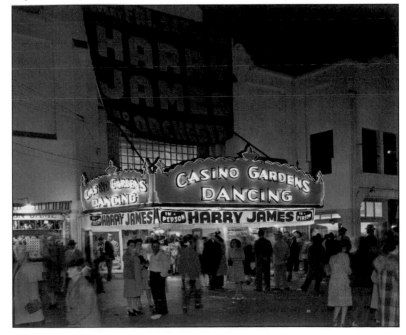

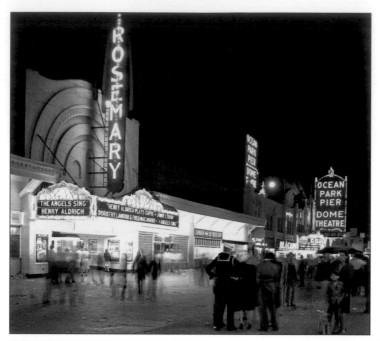

ROSEMARY THEATER, OCEAN PARK PIER. A disastrous fire occurred at the pier in 1924. The Rosemary and Dome theaters, the rides, and the concessions were completely destroyed. The theaters and pier were rebuilt in 1925. The new pier celebrated its grand opening with a 10-day festival beginning on August 29, 1925. One hundred thousand people visited the pier on opening day. (Santa Monica Historical Society Museum, Bill Beebe Collection.)

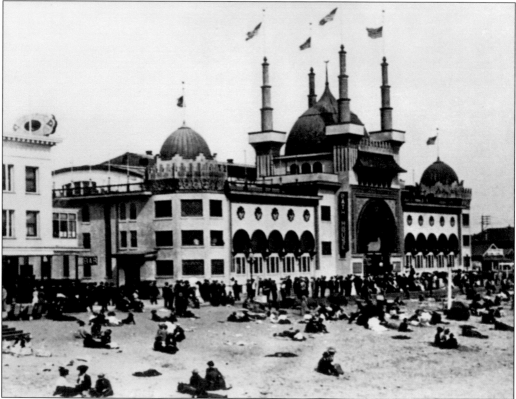

OCEAN PARK BATHHOUSE, C. 1910. This was one of the most elaborate buildings during its day. It was constructed by A. R. Fraser who had been a partner of Abbot Kinney and others in the Ocean Park Improvement Company. (Santa Monica Historical Society Museum, *Outlook* Collection.)

Five

FUN CITY
SPORTS AND THE BEACH

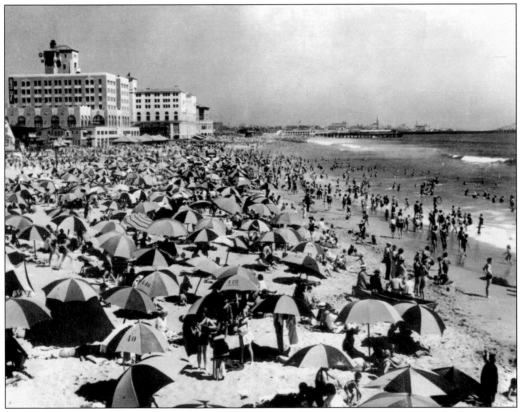

BEACH SCENE, C. 1930S. Santa Monica Beach has always been a popular spot for locals and visitors from all over the world. During the 1920s, exclusive beach clubs were built along the Santa Monica beaches. They included the Santa Monica Athletic Club, Santa Monica Swimming Club, the Deauville, the Beach Club, the Wavecrest, the Edgewater, the Breakers, and the Casa del Mar. During the late 1800s, the auto races started and other popular sports followed, such as golf, tennis, and polo.

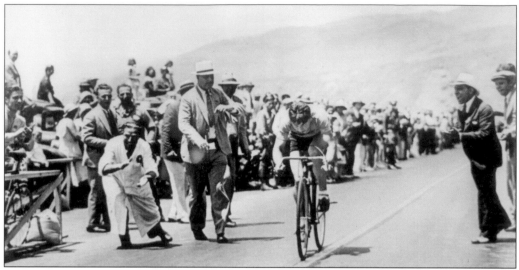

BICYCLE RACE, C. 1930S. The crowd is cheering on this bicyclist as he pedals down the Pacific Coast Highway.

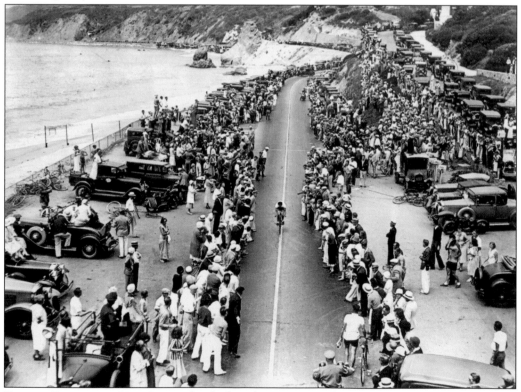

BICYCLE RACES, C. 1930S. Pictured is the bicycle race on Pacific Coast Highway in Santa Monica with hundreds of viewers. A bicycle race on the Fourth of July in 1899 started at Sixth and San Pedro Streets in downtown Los Angeles and ended at Ocean Avenue and Wilshire Boulevard in Santa Monica. Except for Main Street in Los Angeles, all the streets of that day were still unpaved and dusty. There were 110 contestants in that race. (Santa Monica Historical Society Museum, *Outlook* Collection.)

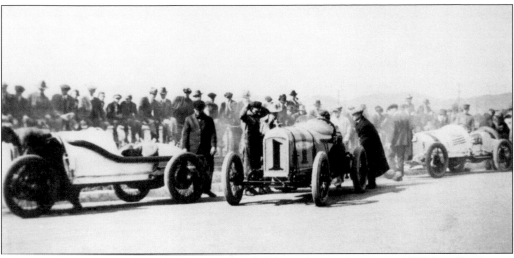

AUTO RACES, EARLY 1900. The race cars headed down Ocean Avenue and Wilshire Boulevard to the Old Soldiers Home and back by way of San Vicente. The fleet of speedsters hurtled and skidded around the track some 30 laps, causing noise and dispersing dust all over Santa Monica. Harris Hanshue won the first race with an average speed of 64.5 miles an hour. The restrictions of World War I brought an end to the races.

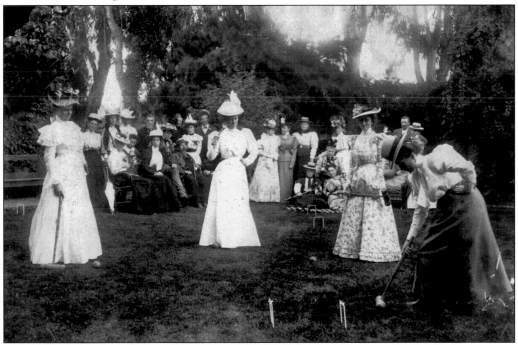

FAMILY MEMBERS OF SEN. JOHN P. JONES PLAYING CROQUET AT MIRAMAR, LATE 1800S. Croquet in America became popular in the late 1800s. Equipment for the sport was advertised in the *New York Clipper* in 1862, and two rule books were published in 1865. In 1867, a New York newspaper editorialized, "Never in the history of outdoor sports in this country had any game achieved so sudden a popularity with both sexes, but especially with the ladies." The American Croquet Association was founded in 1867 to promote the international form of the sport. Croquet ancestry can be traced to the 14th century. (Santa Monica Historical Society Museum, Jones Collection.)

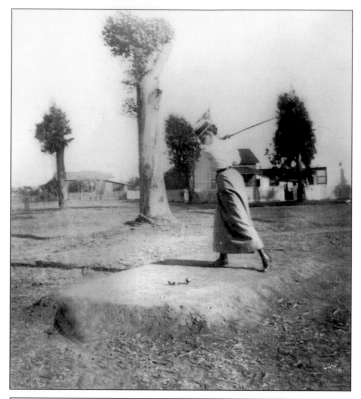

MARION JONES, DAUGHTER OF SENATOR JONES, EARLY 1900S. Marion was an avid sportswoman. She enjoyed golf, croquet, and tennis. She made the Jones family name more resplendent by taking the tennis championship honors five years in a row at the annual Tournament of the South played on the Casino Courts in Santa Monica. Marion went on to the nationals, which she won in 1899 at Philadelphia and again in 1902. Tournaments, tennis, polo races, croquet, bicycle meets, horse races, and swimming contests furnished amusement for the "smart set" and the Sunday crowd. (Santa Monica Historical Society Museum, Jones Collection.)

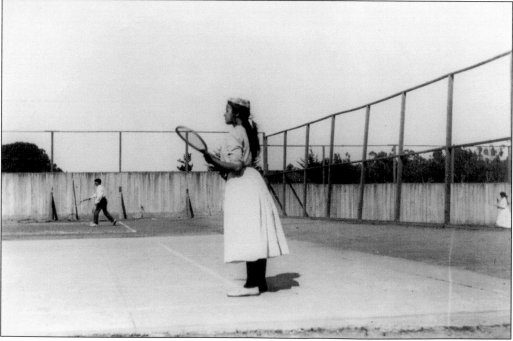

MARION JONES, LATE 1800S. Marion was the first to bring Santa Monica and the Bay District into the national tennis limelight. She captured the national women's singles in 1887 and 1902. (Santa Monica Historical Society Museum, Jones Collection.)

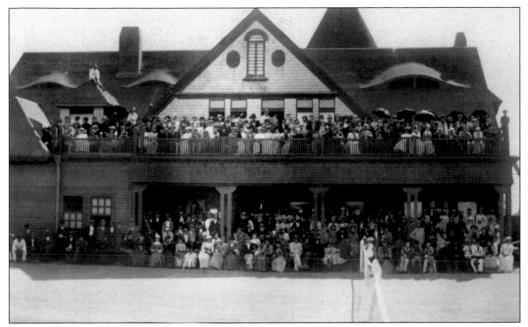

CROWDS OF SPECTATORS AT A TENNIS CLUB AT THIRD STREET AND WILSHIRE BOULEVARD, LATE 1800S. Tennis has carried the fame of Santa Monica further than any other sport. Those to whom the credit belongs for laying the foundation upon which this fame grew in advancing tennis as one of its primary purposes include the Santa Monica Improvement Company, which was incorporated in 1887. It acquired what was known as the Casino property on Third Street and erected a clubhouse. Among the directors of this company were Santa Monica cofounders Senator Jones and Colonel Baker. (Santa Monica Historical Society Museum, Jones Collection.)

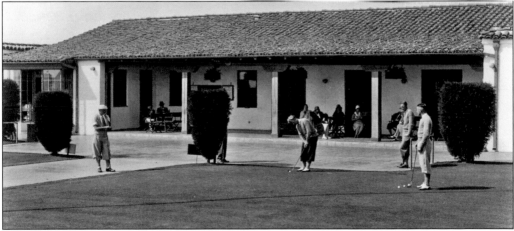

THE CLUBHOUSE FOR SANTA MONICA MUNICIPAL GOLF COURSE AT CLOVER FIELD, 1928. Amateur golf made rapid strides in Santa Monica. Thanks to the teaching of Clover Field Municipal Course professional Lou Berrien, several players of championship caliber were developed. Berrien took special interest in Santa Monica High School boys George Hine and Freddy Gordon, and through his masterful teaching they became champions not only of Santa Monica and the Bay District, but also of Southern California. In 1930, the Santa Monica Junior Chamber of Commerce started a golf tournament at the municipal course. It drew the nation's leading professional stars and most of the coast's top-notch amateurs. (Santa Monica Historical Society Museum, *Outlook* Collection.)

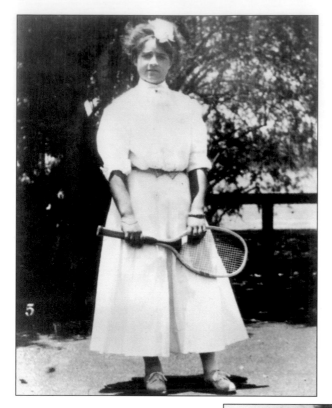

MAY SUTTON BUNDY. For more than half a century, May, Violet, Florence, and Ethel, all sisters from Santa Monica, stood out in the tennis world with their superb sportsmanship. May was the first woman to win the tennis championship at Wimbledon. (Santa Monica Historical Society Museum, *Outlook* Collection.)

GERTRUDE "GUSSIE" MORAN, 1949. Moran was one of Santa Monica's great tennis players. She won five national titles. Her famous lace panties caused Wimbledon its greatest sensation, and the biggest crowds in history packed England's famous Center Court. (Santa Monica Historical Society Museum, *Outlook* Collection.)

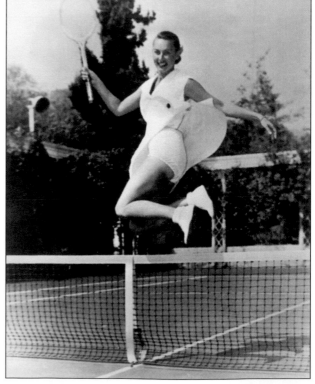

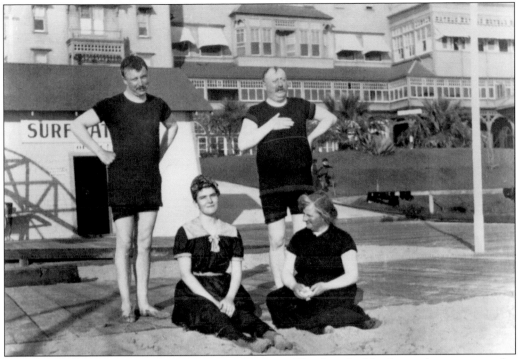

SUNBATHERS AT THE ARCADIA HOTEL, LATE 1800S. The Arcadia Hotel was a long, rectangular 125-room building lying along the edge of the bluffs on Ocean Avenue between what is now Colorado Avenue and Pico Boulevard. On the ocean side, five stories dropped down to the beach. The hotel was considered one of the most elegant on the coast and was a popular place for tourists. (Santa Monica Historical Society Museum, *Outlook* Collection.)

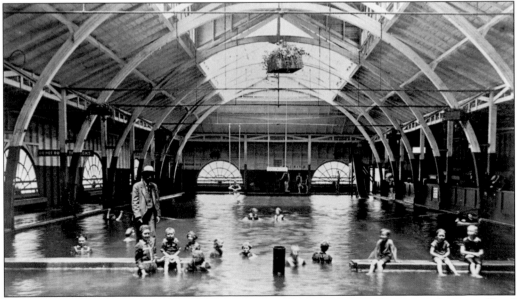

NORTH BEACH BATHHOUSE PLUNGE, LATE 1800S. Youngsters enjoy the warm saltwater offered by the bathhouse plunge. A dip cost 25¢. Visitors often watched bathers from the side bleachers. (Santa Monica Historical Society Museum, *Outlook* Collection.)

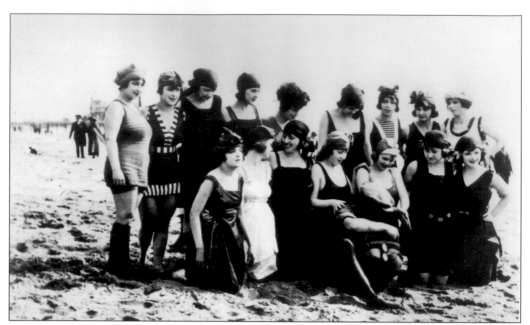

BATHING BEAUTIES AT SANTA MONICA BEACH, 1920. During the 1920s and early 1930s, bathing-suit contests were held often in Ocean Park and Santa Monica. The bathers wore more comfortable swimwear than what was available in the 1890s, which consisted of woolen suits that covered most of the body. Movie studios filmed bathing beauties on the beach as well as in other scenes.

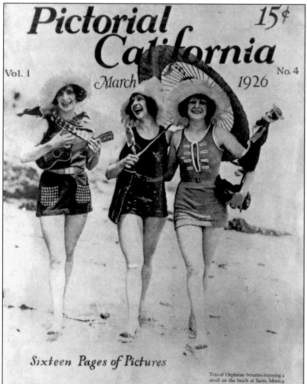

ORPHEUM BEAUTIES, MARCH 1926. On the cover of *Pictorial California* magazine is a troupe of Orpheum beauties enjoying a stroll on the beach at Santa Monica.

A Beauty Contest, c. 1930.
Contests were often held at the beach in the early days. (Santa Monica Historical Society Museum, *Outlook* Collection.)

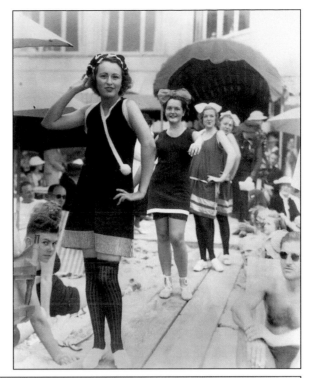

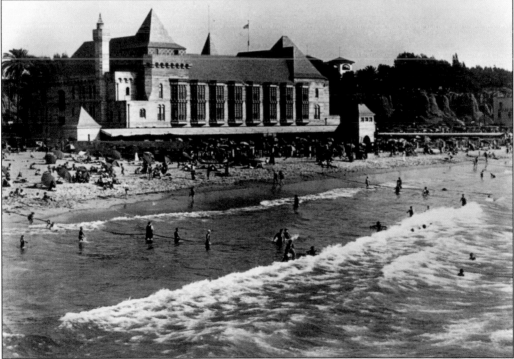

Deauville Club, 1920s. The magnificent Deauville beach club was built on the site of the old North Beach Bathhouse (north of Santa Monica Pier). It was inspired by the famous club in Deauville, France.

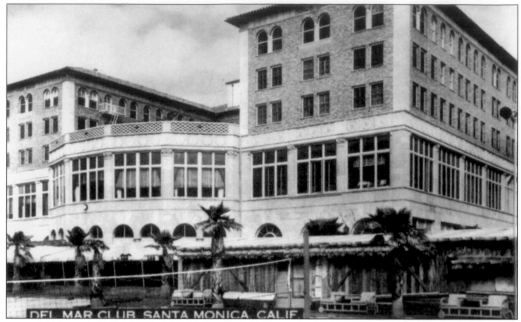

DEL MAR CLUB. On May 1, 1926, E. A. and T. D. Harter opened what immediately would become the grand dame of Santa Monica. They spared no expense in building this beach club for the then incredible sum of $2 million. Casa Del Mar attracted leading business executives and Hollywood celebrities. The club was renowned for its swinging parties, festive affairs, family-oriented swim meets, and other events.

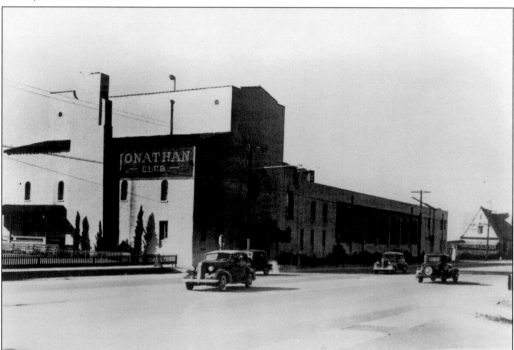

JONATHAN CLUB. Located at 850 Palisades Beach Road, this private beach club was originally built in 1926 as the Sea Breeze Club.

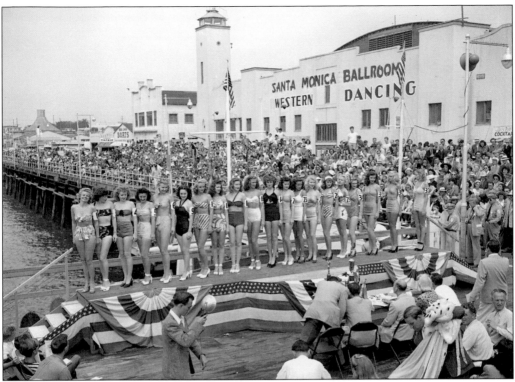

BEAUTY CONTESTANTS, 1940s. A crowd of spectators watches a bathing-beauty contest held by the Santa Monica Ballroom, formerly the La Monica Ballroom, on the Santa Monica Pier. (Santa Monica Historical Society Museum, Bill Beebe Collection.)

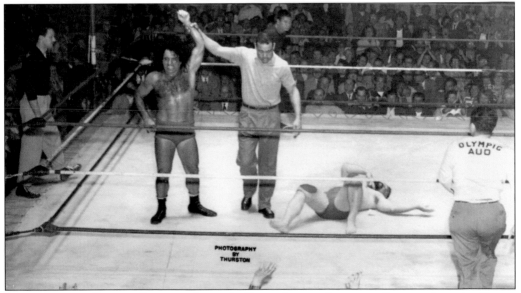

BARON MICHEL LEONE. Renowned wrestler Baron Leone wins a wrestling match at the Ocean Park Arena. Former world heavyweight champion Joe Louis is raising Baron Leone's hand. Leone was also one of the Muscle Beach athletes. He lived in Ocean Park with his wife, Billie, for many years. (Courtesy Billie Leone.)

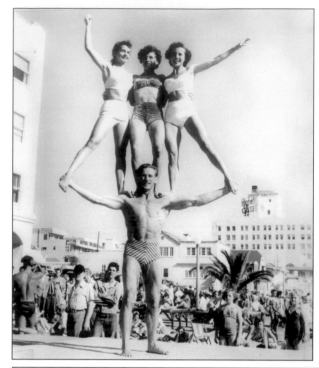

MUSCLE BEACH PERFORMERS, 1940s. At Muscle Beach, there might be three or more acts performed simultaneously on the platform. At the same time, one could watch gymnasts showing their skills on the bars or performing somersaults from the rings. Men and women would also balance on top of each other like human pyramids. Muscle Beach was located just south of Santa Monica Pier. (Courtesy Glenn Sunby.)

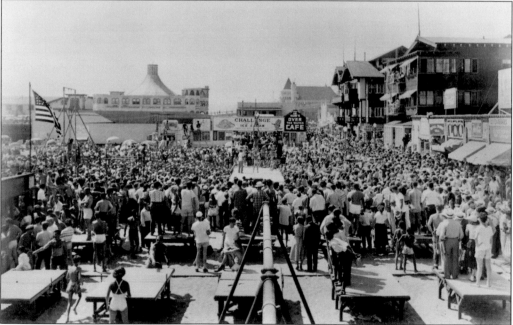

MUSCLE BEACH. Pictured is Muscle Beach in its heyday, around 1948, with hundreds of spectators. Some of the great acrobats and body builders who performed here were Harold Zinkin (first Mr. California), Jack LaLanne, Vic Tanny, Russ Saunders, Baron Michel Leone, Pudgy and Les Stockton, Glenn Sunby, Paula Unger Boelsems, and Joe Gold of Gold's Gym. Santa Monica Beach was a magnet for fitness leaders around the world. (Santa Monica Historical Society Museum, Bill Beebe Collection.)

A MUSCLE BEACH ATHLETE IS FLANKED BY TWO ADMIRERS AS HE FLEXES HIS MUSCLES, 1950. Weight lifting and bodybuilding as popular spectacle sport came to the beach after World War II. During the 1930s, several people brought their own weights and both men and women used them to build up their strength as a means to accomplish acrobatic routines. A popular place for training was Gold's Gym. Bodybuilders from everywhere, including Arnold Schwarzenegger, trained at the gym. Santa Monican Paula Unger Boelsems progressed from a little eight-year-old, begging people to teach her tricks, to one of the most graceful and top athletes at Muscle Beach. (Santa Monica Historical Society Museum, Beebe Collection.)

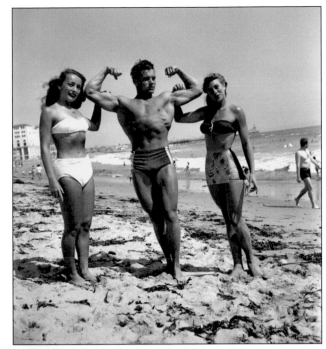

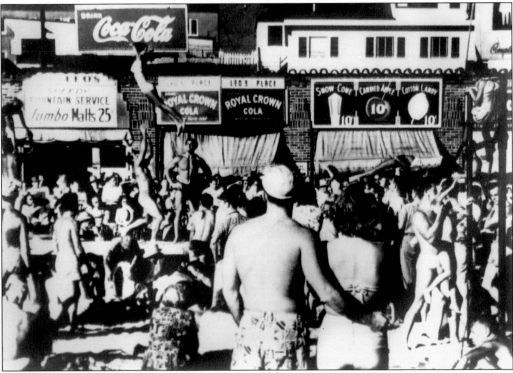

MUSCLE BEACH PERFORMERS, 1950s. During the 1930s, the country was in the Great Depression and money was scarce and many were unemployed. After World War II, similar circumstances occurred. Most people who lived in and around the area spent their weekends at the beach. Muscle Beach provided lots of exciting free entertainment. It closed down in the late 1950s.

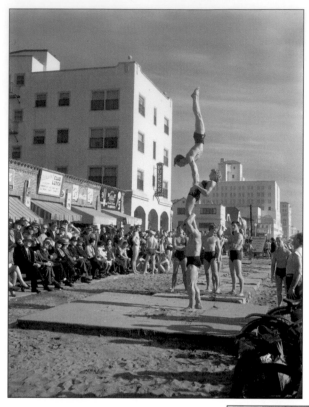

MUSCLE BEACH PERFORMERS, 1940. Located just south of Santa Monica Pier, Muscle Beach was started in the early 1930s. Within 20 years, it turned into an extraordinary entertainment with performances before thousands of spectators. (Santa Monica Historical Society Museum, Bill Beebe Collection.)

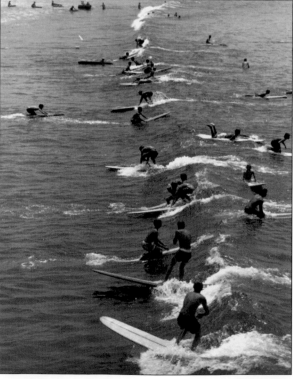

SURFERS. Surfing was beginning to sweep the California coast in the early 1940s. These surfers are north of Santa Monica Pier.

Six

BUSINESSES
A TOWN AT WORK

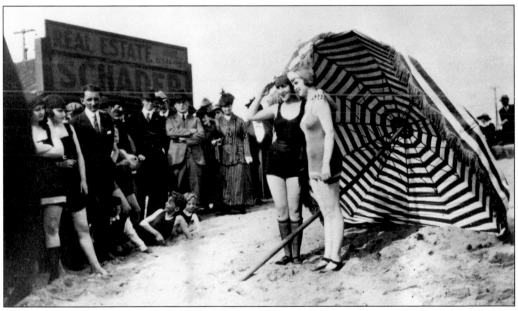

REAL ESTATE PROMOTERS, 1907. These bathing beauties were used to attract prospective buyers to a Shader Real Estate promotion for Santa Monica beachfront property. Businesses really started to grow when the trains brought potential land owners and tourists to Santa Monica in the late 1800s. By 1924, Santa Monica had its first department store, Hensheys. Before that, people did most of their major shopping in Los Angeles. The Third Street Mall and Santa Monica Boulevard became the main shopping areas. During World War II, people came from different parts of the country to work at the Douglas Aircraft plant. Santa Monica's population skyrocketed, and a big change came over Santa Monica. Business increased, real estate was selling, and the hotel industry was at an all-time high. (Courtesy Elliott Welsh.)

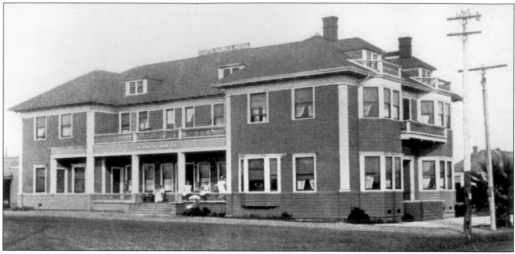

SANTA MONICA HOTEL, C. 1875. The hotel was originally established as a rooming house for the John P. Jones wharf workers in 1878. This building eventually became the city's first major hotel. Georgina Jones and her three daughters lived at the hotel while waiting for Miramar to be completed. The Santa Monica Historical Society Museum has a guest book from this hotel with the "Jones" signature.

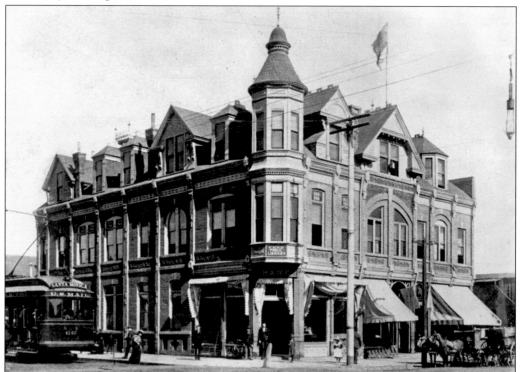

BANK OF SANTA MONICA. The bank was located on Third Street in the late 1800s. Santa Monica Library's first location was on the second floor. In the 1890s, the Women's Christian Temperance Union, which established a reading room in 1885, donated its entire library of 800 volumes to the city. From leading citizens, the city appointed a board of library directors. The committee rented two rooms in the Bank of Santa Monica.

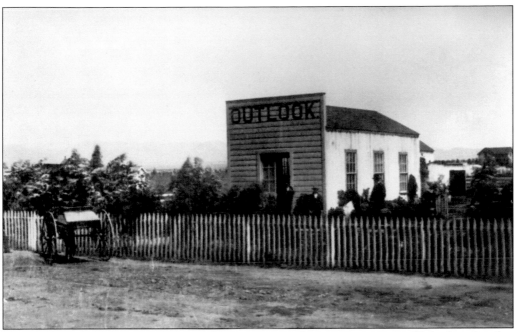

OUTLOOK NEWSPAPER. The first issue of Santa Monica's first newspaper was published on October 13, 1875, in a small wooden building. Its editor was L. T. Fisher. This edition recorded the growth the town had experienced since the first lot sale. The newspaper had its ups and downs over the years. In 1895, the *Outlook* went from a weekly to a daily newspaper. On March 14, 1998, the *Outlook* ceased publication because of a decline in revenue. (Santa Monica Historical Society Museum, *Outlook*/Smith Collection.)

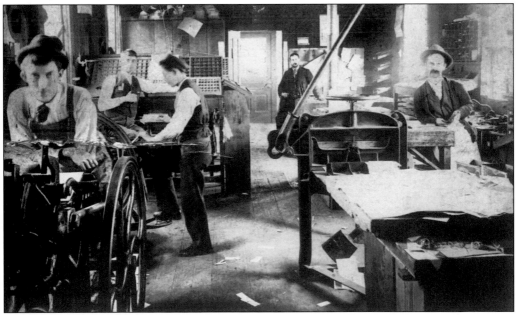

EARLY NEWSPAPER SHOP, C. 1898. Printing equipment in the early days of the *Outlook*, pictured here, was primitive compared to modern high-speed typesetters and presses. (Santa Monica Historical Society Museum, *Outlook*/Smith Collection.)

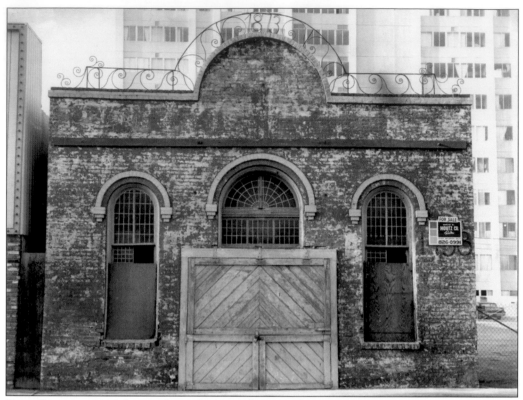

RAPP SALOON, 1875. Located at 1438 Second Street, this was the first masonry structure in the city, owned by William Rapp. It was used as Santa Monica's town hall from May 1888 to February 1889 and housed a Salvation Army meeting hall, radiator repair shop, art galleries, and storage for the Vitagraph Film Company, which was one of the first movie studios in Santa Monica. The landmark building still stands today; American Youth Hostel owns the property. (Santa Monica Historical Society Museum, *Outlook* Collection.)

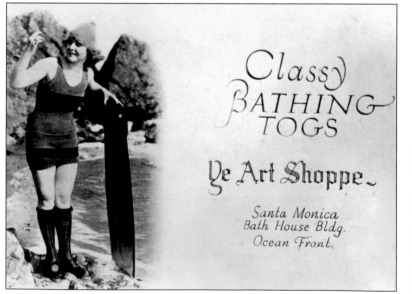

BATHING SUITS FOR SALE, C. 1920. In this advertisement, Ye Art Shoppe is catching the eye of potential buyers for its "classy bathing togs." (Courtesy Elliott Welsh.)

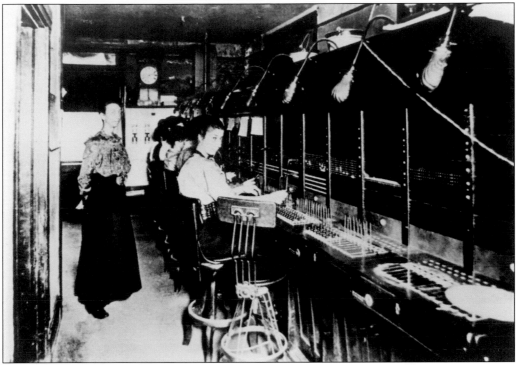

YOUR CALL PLEASE. Early Santa Monica subscribers to the Home Telephone and Telegraph Company, which evolved into General Telephone, might have spoken to one of these operators watched over by a supervisor in this 1909 photograph. Unless one had service from two competing telephone firms, one could not talk across town. (Santa Monica Historical Society Museum, *Outlook* Collection.)

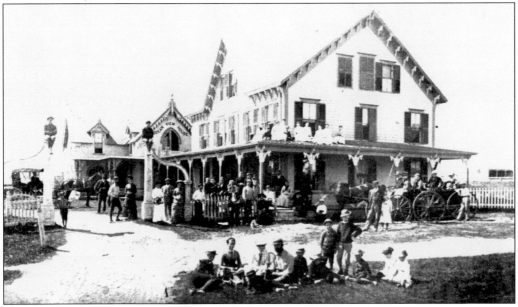

OCEAN VIEW HOUSE, C. 1900. This hotel overlooked Palisades Park and Ocean Avenue. It had an incredible ocean view. (Courtesy Santa Monica Public Library Image Archives.)

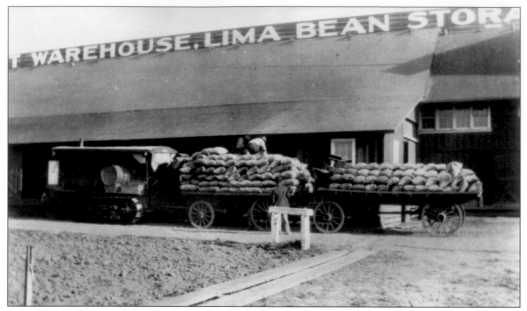

Lima Bean Warehouse, c. 1916. Charles J. Haines operated this warehouse, which dispensed hay, grain, feed, flour, and coal. Mainly it was a storage point for lima beans, which were a major product of Santa Monica in those days. In this photograph, a tractor hauls two wagon loads of beans to the warehouse located at what is now Eighteenth Street and Colorado Avenue. (Courtesy Donald Howland.)

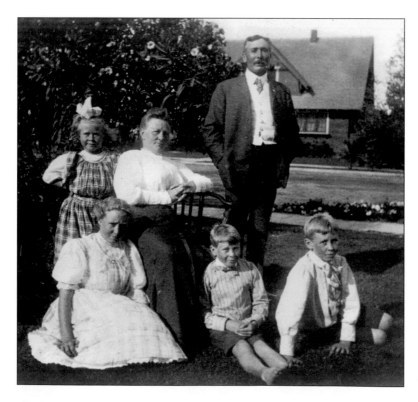

The Charles A. Tegner Family. Charles A. Tegner and his wife, Emma, are pictured here with their children Edla (standing), Thelma, Carl (sitting on the right), and Hilding. Tegner was born in Sweden. He came to Santa Monica in 1887 and was engaged in a variety of business enterprises. Tegner was the builder and owner of the first theater in the city, the Majestic, and the first department store, Hensheys. (Courtesy Virginia Tegner Spurgin.)

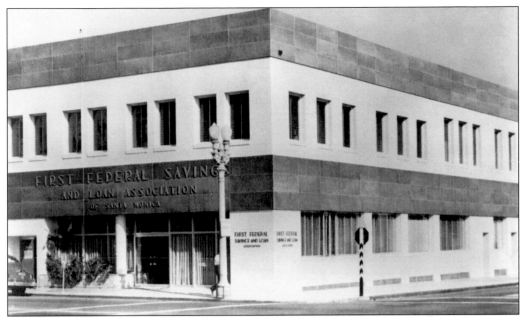

FIRST FEDERAL BANK. In 1921, the bank was called Citizens Guarantee Building and Loan Association, and one of the founders was Dr. William S. Mortensen. In 1935, the company name changed to First Federal Savings and Loan. In 1955, William S. Mortensen, grandson of the founder, started working at First Federal. In 1983, the company changed to a savings bank. This early location was at Santa Monica Boulevard and Second Street.

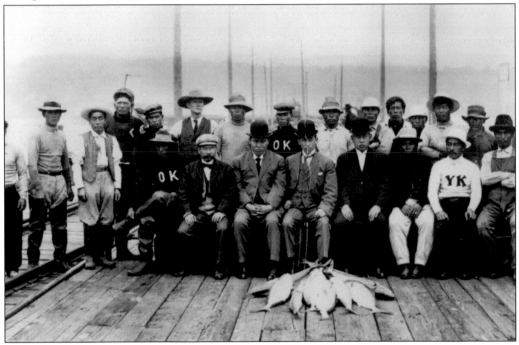

JAPANESE FISHING VILLAGE. About 300 Japanese fishermen and their families established a village north of the Long Wharf. The livelihood of the villagers was dependent on the catch from Santa Monica Bay. Fire destroyed the village in 1916.

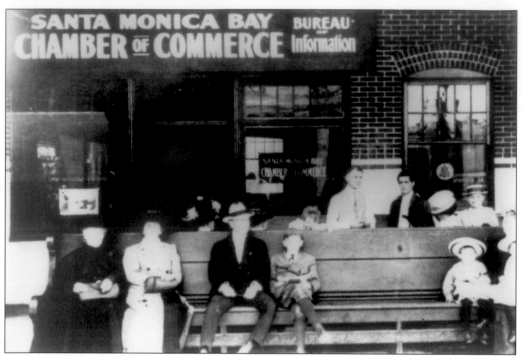

SANTA MONICA BAY CHAMBER OF COMMERCE. The chamber was incorporated on May 20, 1925. It was an outgrowth of the Santa Monica-Ocean Park Association of Commerce, which operated informally from around 1911 to 1925. The main broad purposes of the Santa Monica Bay Chamber of Commerce are to promote and protect the business interests of the community, to assist and encourage the continued growth and development of the city, and to make Santa Monica an even finer place in which to live.

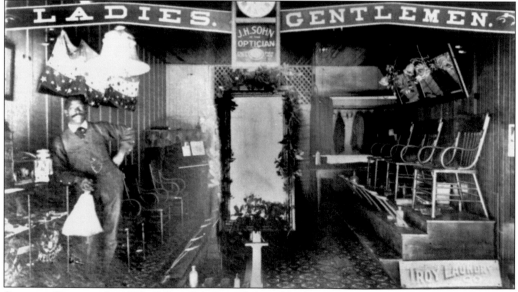

SHINING PARLOR. In 1907, Gilbert McCarroll, possibly the city's first black businessman, opened his "Shining Parlor" on Pier Avenue. Both ladies and gentlemen were urged off the wood-sidewalk avenue to sit in his fully equipped parlor and have their shoes shined.

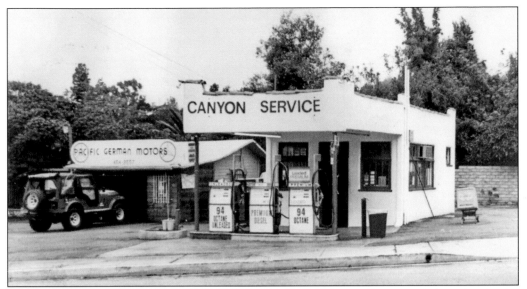

CANYON SERVICE STATION. The station, located in Santa Monica Canyon, is believed to be the oldest operating station in Los Angeles County. It was constructed in 1928 by Perfecto Marquez of the original land-grant family of the canyon. (Courtesy Angie Marquez Olivera.)

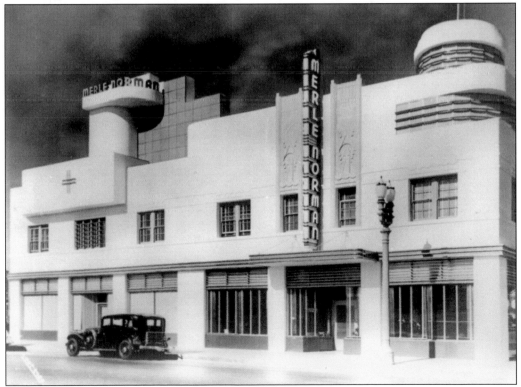

MERLE NORMAN BUILDING. This building is located at 2627 Main Street. It was used by Merle Norman for her Merle Norman Cosmetic Company. A famed cosmetics entrepreneur, Norman began the business in her Ocean Park home. Upon her death, the business was then taken over by her nephew, J. B. Nethercutt, who was her chief chemist.

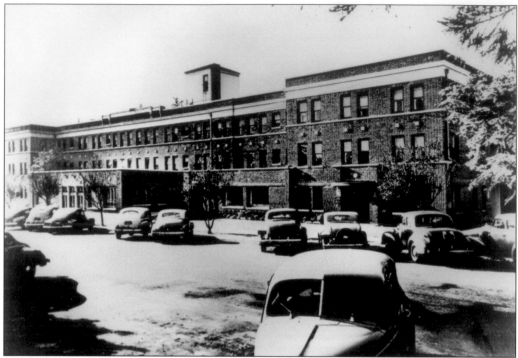

SANTA MONICA HOSPITAL. This 60-bed hospital was established in 1926 by physicians William Mortensen and August Hromadka. In the early years, Mortensen and Hromadka did most of their work at Loamshire Hospital. The physicians saw the need for a larger, more modern hospital as the city grew. They secured property for the hospital and raised the money for its construction. In recent years, it has become the Santa Monica-UCLA Medical Center. (Courtesy Santa Monica Hospital.)

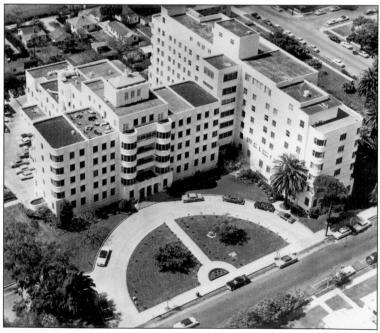

SAINT JOHN'S HEALTH CENTER. Located at 1328 Twenty-second Street, this hospital was established by the Sisters of Charity of Leavenworth, Kansas. Construction began on the hospital in 1939. In 1942, the 87-bed hospital named for St. John the Apostle opened its doors. (Courtesy Saint John's Health Center.)

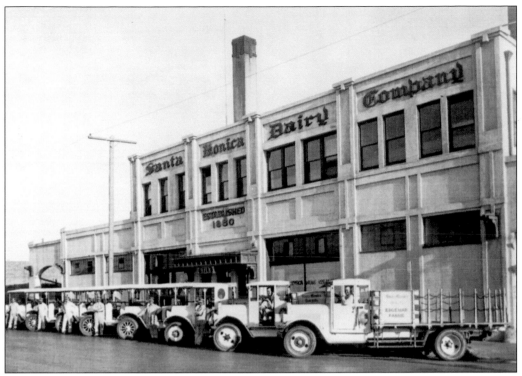

SANTA MONICA DAIRY COMPANY. In 1887 at age 20, Herman Michel bought out Charles Hawes's dairy at Seventeenth Street and Santa Monica Boulevard. He had 45 cows in a corral just off the boulevard. As the business expanded, the dairy was moved to the Ballona Creek area, where the dairyman purchased 1,000 acres of land. The company name was later changed to Edgemar Farms. Michel sold his herd in 1947.

SANTA MONICA DAIRY COMPANY BOTTLING PLANT, EARLY 1900S. The Santa Monica Dairy Company was owned by Herman Michel. In 1925, he entered politics and on his first attempt was elected mayor of Santa Monica, serving two terms. He also served as president of the chamber of commerce.

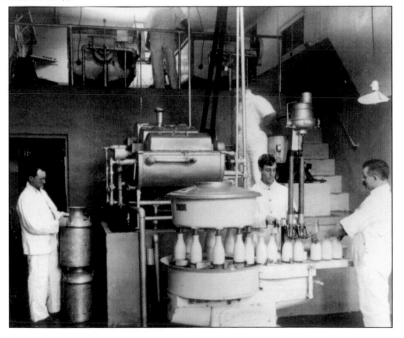

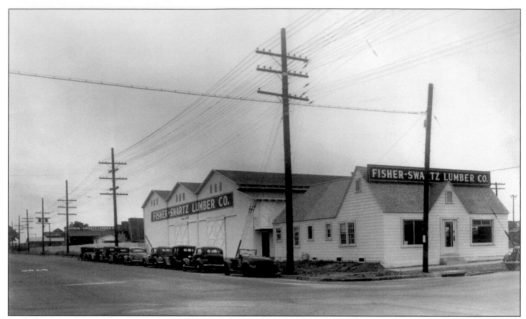

FISHER LUMBER COMPANY. Founded in 1923, Fisher Lumber was one of the oldest continually operated businesses in Santa Monica in the same location. Originally named Fisher-Swartz Lumber Company after its owners, the name changed to Fisher when Swartz left the company in 1944. The building was sold to the City of Santa Monica in 2005. The company is now Fisher Hardware and Lumber, located at 1600 Lincoln Boulevard.

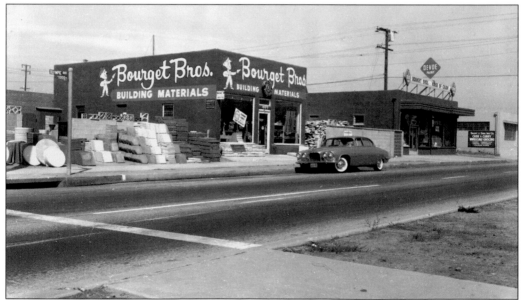

BOURGET BROTHERS. This business is located at 1646 Eleventh Street. The three Bourget brothers, Leo, Larry, and Henry, started the business in 1947 after serving in World War II. They started out with $300 and manufactured masonry blocks and landscaping and building materials. They now manufacture lumber as well. Today the large company is run by younger members of the family—John Bourget and Leonard Bourget. All of the Bourgets are native Santa Monicans. (Courtesy Bourget Brothers.)

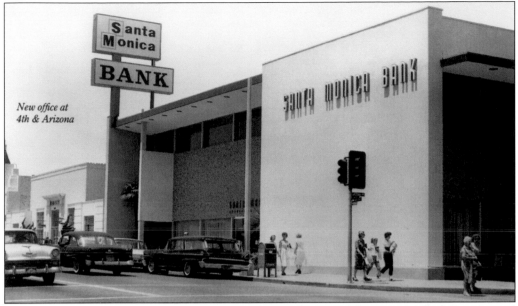

SANTA MONICA BANK. Aubrey E. Austin, president and owner of the Santa Monica Commercial and Savings Bank from 1933 to the date of his death in 1949, helped with the growth and development of Santa Monica. Aubrey E. Austin Jr. began in his father's bank in the mid-1940s and filled positions from messenger to president. The bank was sold to Western Bank in 1998, which sold it to U.S. Bank a year later. (Courtesy Santa Monica Bank.)

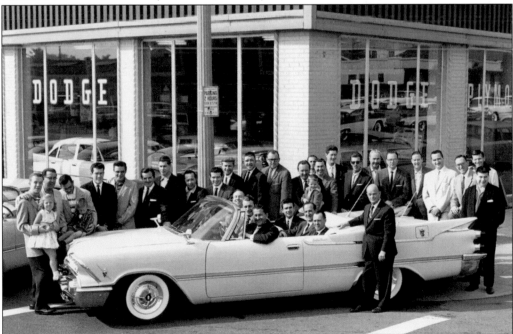

LAWRENCE WELK IN HIS NEW DODGE, C. 1958. Musician Lawrence Welk is pictured sitting in the driver's seat of his new Dodge; Kenneth Parr is directly behind him and Claude Short, owner of the dealership, is standing by the side of the automobile. Dodge Dealers of Southern California sponsored the Welk Show at Lick Pier in Ocean Park.

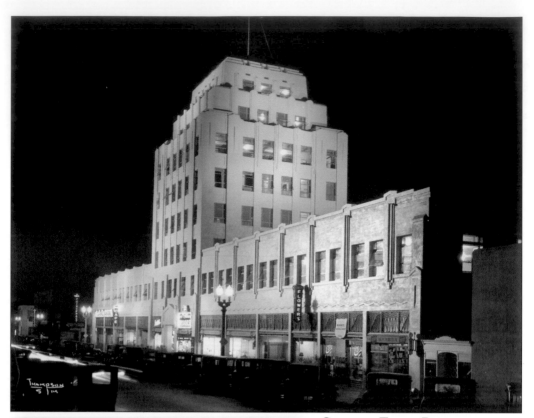

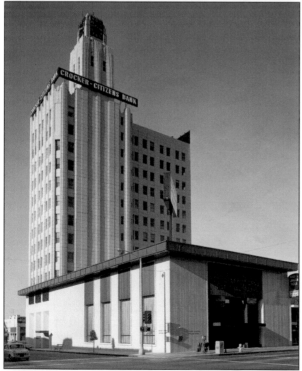

CENTRAL TOWER BUILDING.
Built in 1929, this eight-story
building, located at 1424 Fourth
Street, was constructed by A. P.
Creel and designed by architect
Eugene Durfee. This site was once
the home of Williamson D. Vawter,
who in 1887 established the city's
first transportation system, a horse-
drawn car line that ran from Ocean
Park to the Soldier's Home in
West Los Angeles. (Santa Monica
Historical Society Museum,
Outlook Collection.)

CROCKER BANK. The building,
known as the Bay Cities Building,
opened in 1929 at 225 Santa Monica
Boulevard. It was designed by
architect Stiles O. Clements. The
clock on the art deco tower is a
downtown landmark.

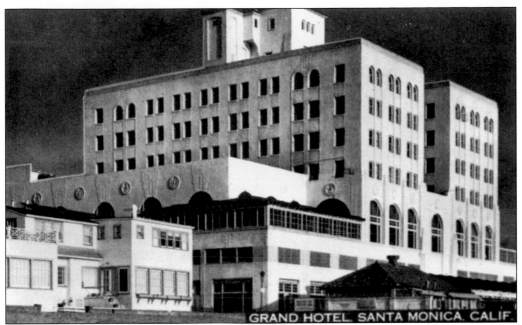

GRAND HOTEL, SEA CASTLE. Originally constructed as the Breakers Beach Club in 1926, it soon became the Grand Hotel. It was also known as the Chase and Monica Hotels before being converted to apartments in the early 1960s and renamed the Sea Castle.

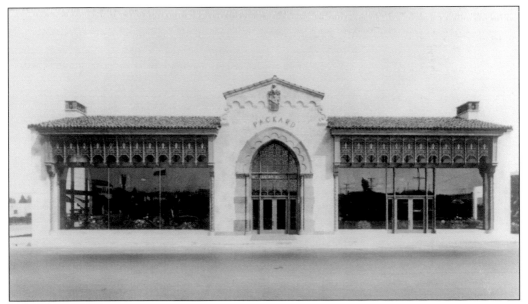

W. I. SIMONSON, MERCEDES BENZ. The Packard Building was constructed in 1936 by W. I. Simonson at Wilshire Boulevard and Sixteenth Street. It was destroyed by fire in the 1980s and rebuilt to its original architecture. At that time, the business was owned by William and Mary Rehwald. In 2005, Sonic Corporation purchased the dealership.

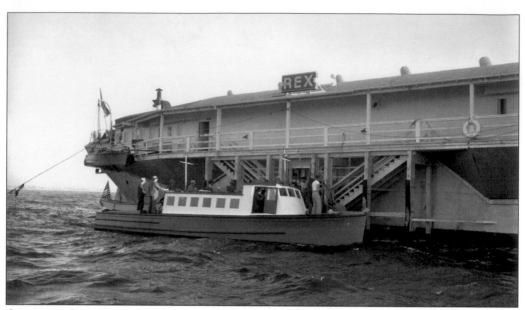

GAMBLING SHIP REX. The *Rex* was a luxurious gambling boat that began operations on May 1, 1938, from its anchorage just over three miles from Santa Monica Beach. Hundreds of patrons were shuttled to the *Rex* on water taxis from the Santa Monica Pier. Tony Conero was owner of the *Rex*. (Santa Monica Historical Society Museum, Bill Beebe Collection.)

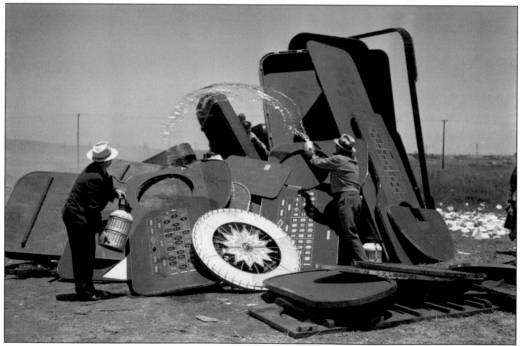

GAMBLING SHIP REX, C. 1940. Sheriff's deputies destroy all the gambling equipment from the gambling ship *Rex*, anchored in the Santa Monica Bay. The raid was led by California attorney general Earl Warren after the courts ruled that the *Rex* was a public nuisance. Conero then took all of his action to Las Vegas, where he later died of a heart attack. (Santa Monica Historical Society Museum, Bill Beebe Collection.)

Seven

A Shopper's Paradise

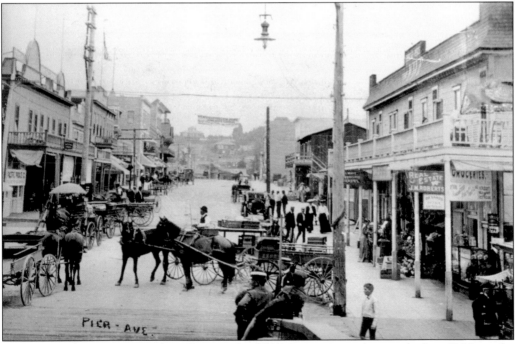

HORSE-AND-BUGGY DAYS. This photograph of Pier Avenue was taken in the late 1800s as the business and shopping area was beginning to grow. By the 1920s, businesses flourished when trains brought thousands of people to Santa Monica. Ocean Park was developing. Santa Monica had its first department store, Hensheys, and its first theater, the Majestic (now called Mayfair). The Third Street Mall and Santa Monica Boulevard attracted many shoppers and tourists. Over the years, many of the hotels and other businesses have been operating successfully.

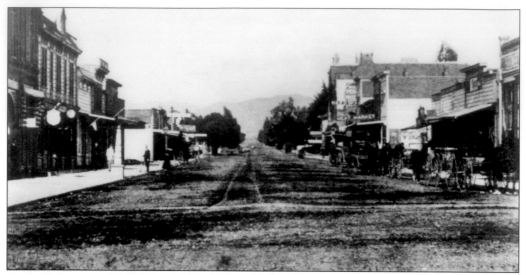

THIRD STREET, C. 1891. This is Third Street looking north from Broadway. The streets had not yet been paved. By 1888, a hotel and theater had been built at the northeast corner of Third Street and Broadway and, within the next five years, two of the city's three early commercial buildings were constructed on the street. (Santa Monica Historical Society Museum, *Outlook* Collection.)

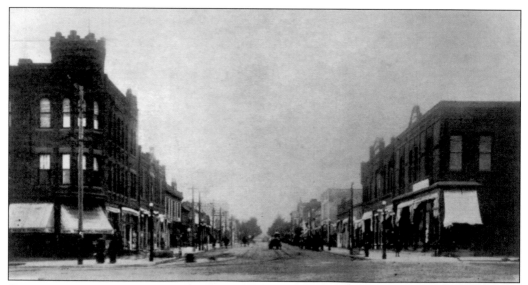

THIRD STREET AND BROADWAY. This is how the street looked in the late 1800s. The building on the left corner is the Keller Building, which still stands today. Second Street is the oldest commercial street in Santa Monica. In the late 1880s, it had a saloon, movie studio, post office, drug store, restaurant, and hotel. In the next decade, Third Street functioned as the city's principal commercial street.

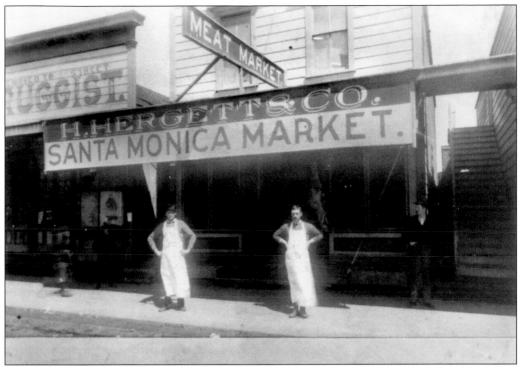

SANTA MONICA MARKET. In 1890, two employees of H. Hergett's Company meat market proudly pose outside their establishment located on Third Street in the heart of Santa Monica's business district. The sidewalk in front of the store had just been paved by the new city government. (Santa Monica Historical Society Museum, *Outlook* Collection.)

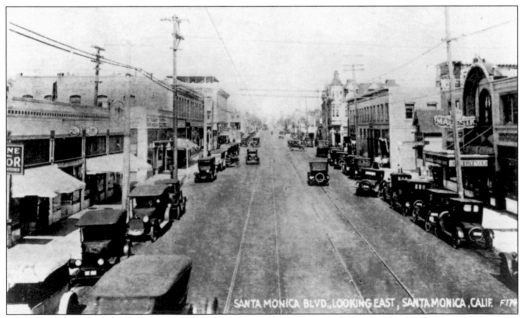

SANTA MONICA BOULEVARD, 1920S. Looking east from Second Street, note the Majestic Theater (now called the Mayfair) located at 214 Santa Monica Boulevard.

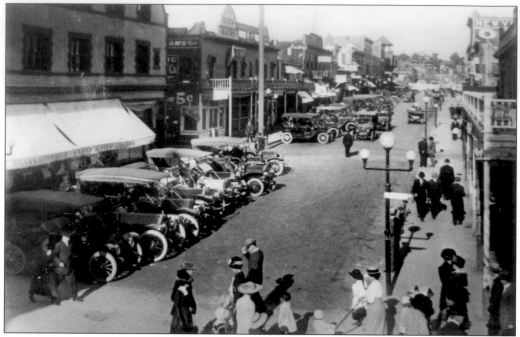

Pier Avenue Shopping and Business Area, Early 1900s. Townspeople of Ocean Park are all dressed up in their finest as they stroll and shop along the avenue. (Santa Monica Historical Society Museum, *Outlook* Collection.)

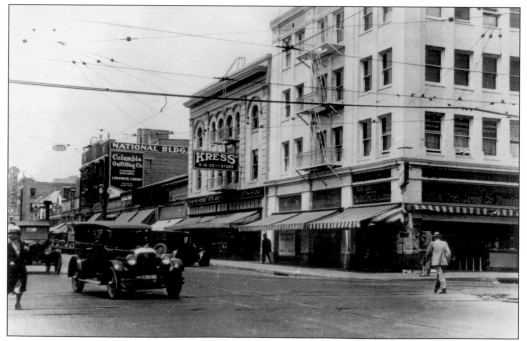

Third Street and Santa Monica Boulevard, c. 1920. In 1905, the Third Street commercial district was between Broadway and Wilshire Boulevard. Along this stretch is the Criterion Theater (at far left), built in 1923 and still operating today. (Santa Monica Historical Society Museum, *Outlook* Collection.)

THIRD STREET, LATE 1930S.
Looking north, the Criterion
Theater's tall sign is visible on
the right side. The business area
was rapidly developing, and Third
Street was becoming a major
shopping area. (Santa Monica
Historical Society Museum,
Outlook Collection.)

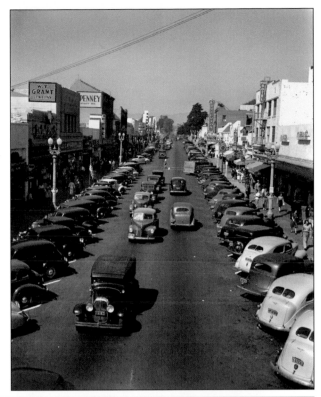

W. T. GRANT COMPANY The
store opened June 4, 1937, on
Third Street, and early arrivers
line up waiting to enter. The sign
on the marquee states, "25¢, 50¢,
and $1.00 Department Stores."
Those were the good old days.
(Santa Monica Historical Society
Museum, Bill Beebe Collection.)

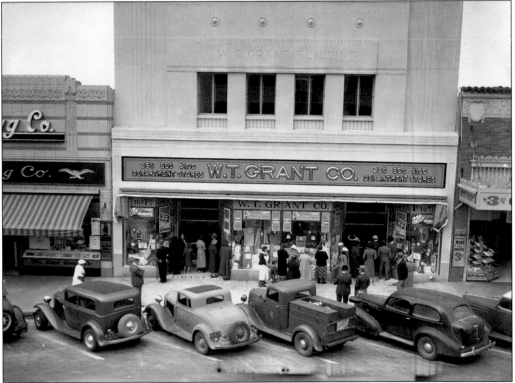

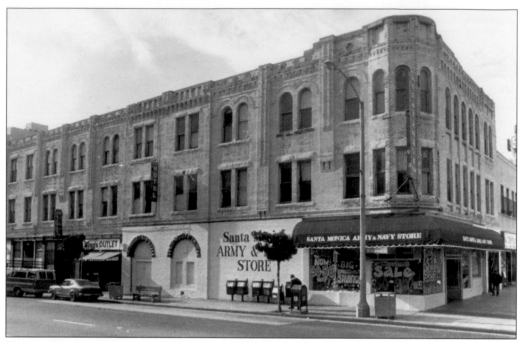

KELLER BUILDING. Built in 1892 by Henry W. Keller, the three-story brick building is located at Third Street and Broadway. It was used originally as a hotel over the ground-floor stores. The building still stands today.

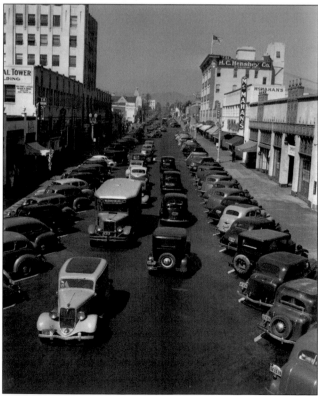

FOURTH STREET SHOPPING AREA, LATE 1930s. Looking north, on the right side of the picture, are McMahan's furniture and Hensheys—both major stores. The Central Tower building is on the left. All parking spaces are filled on both sides of the street. Parking spaces were even scarce in those days. Fourth Street, between Wilshire Boulevard and Colorado Avenue, was the third major downtown street to be developed in the city; it was residential until the early 1920s. (Santa Monica Historical Society Museum, *Outlook* Collection.)

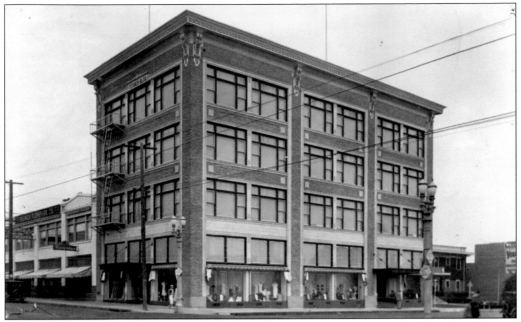

HENSHEYS DEPARTMENT STORE, 1924. Built by Charles E. Tegner and designed by architect Henry C. Hollwedel, this four-story brick building was Santa Monica's first department store. In 1962, the brick facade was covered with a metal screen to provide a modern-looking exterior. Hensheys is no longer in business; it closed in July 1992.

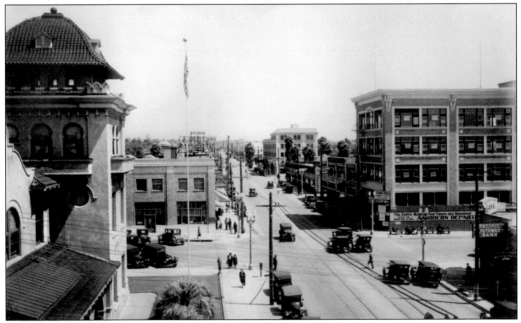

SANTA MONICA BOULEVARD AND FOURTH STREET, 1930S. Looking east, note the first city hall on the left and Hensheys Department Store (tall building) on the right. Formerly known as Oregon Avenue, Santa Monica Boulevard was the city's early arterial street and the principal access route from Los Angeles in the 1920s. It was designated as U.S. Highway 66, which began in Chicago and ended in Santa Monica.

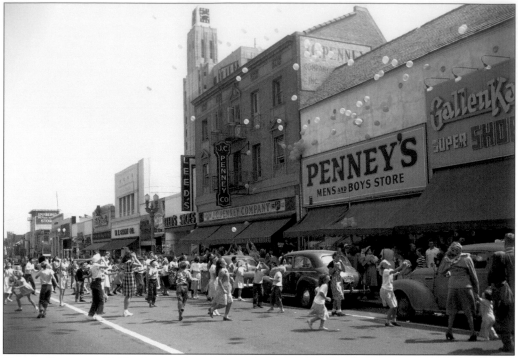

THIRD STREET, 1948. A crowd is chasing balloons in front of Penney's Mens and Boys Store in a promotion for a Penney's sale. (Santa Monica Historical Society Museum, Bill Beebe Collection.)

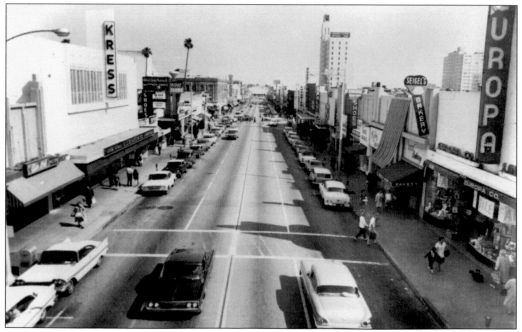

THIRD STREET, C. 1950. This view looking south from Wilshire Boulevard shows the names of many shops that are no longer there today. The street was closed to vehicular traffic in 1965 and became a pedestrian mall.

Eight

CELEBRITIES AND THE GOLD COAST

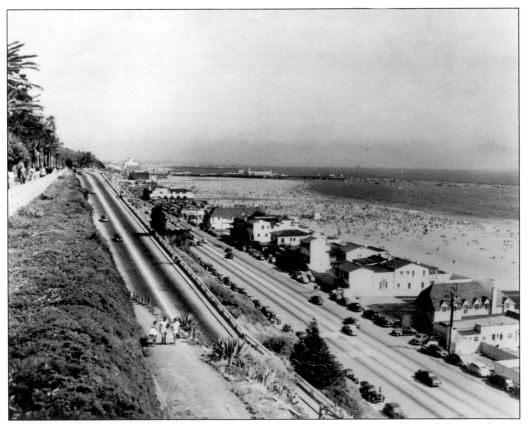

THE GOLD COAST, C. 1940. The Gold Coast was given that name because of the number of wealthy and famous motion-picture celebrities who owned or occupied homes along this section of the oceanfront. The most palatial home along the Gold Coast was that of Marion Davies, built for her in the late 1920s by her companion, newspaper magnate William Randolph Hearst. The property had over 100 rooms, a vast swimming pool lined in Italian marble, and tennis courts.

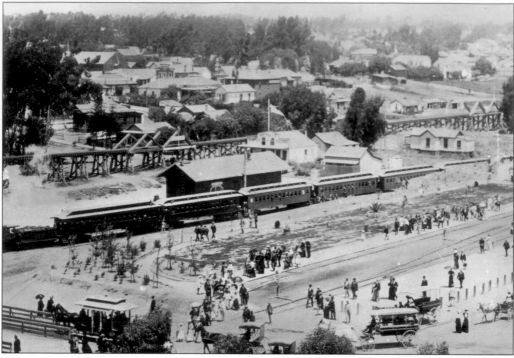

KALEM FILM COMPANY. In this photograph are the Southern Pacific rail yards in Santa Monica, *c.* 1907. The film company was located where Colorado Avenue and Fourth Street are today. In 1911, the Kalem Film Company opened its studio in and around a carbarn seen at the far left of this photograph, partially obscured by the train. (Courtesy Marc Wanamaker/Bison Archives.)

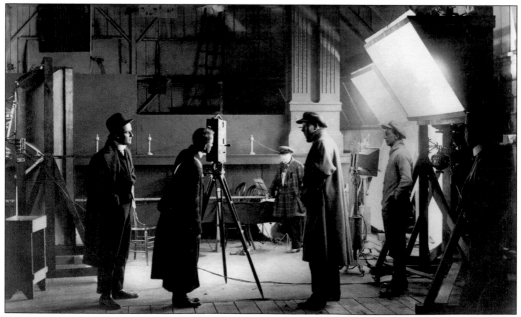

KALEM FILM SET. In 1914, this filming was done by Kalem Company in Santa Monica at their Southern Pacific rail yard location. Director Marshall Neilan is seen at left directing a "Ham and Bud" comedy. (Courtesy Marc Wanamaker/Bison Archives.)

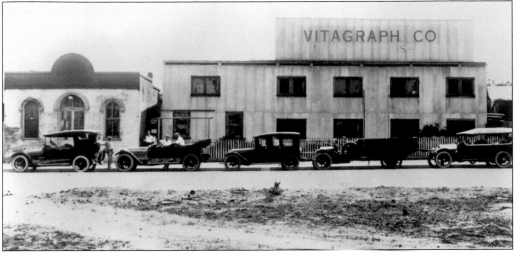

VITAGRAPH FILM COMPANY. Santa Monica's first movie studio, Vitagraph Company, filmed about one western a week after its establishment in 1910. The studio helped develop the careers of Charlie Chaplin, Rudolph Valentino, and Mary Pickford. It was located on Second Street next to the Rapp Saloon, a Santa Monica landmark. (Courtesy Marc Wanamaker/Bison Archives.)

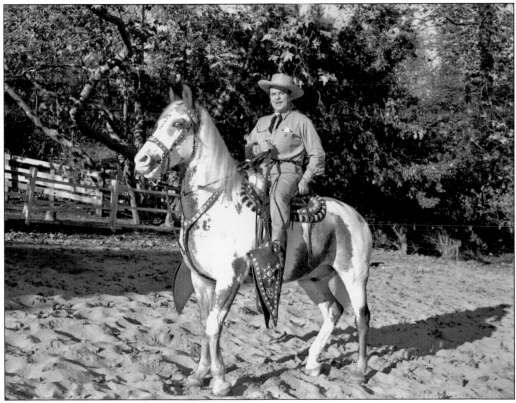

LEO CARRILLO. A famous actor, Leo was the son of Juan J. Carrillo, the first police judge and, for many years, a Santa Monica City trustee. The Carrillos were one of California's first families. Leo grew up in Santa Monica and in later years attained fame and fortune on the stage and screen. (Santa Monica Historical Society Museum, Bill Beebe Collection.)

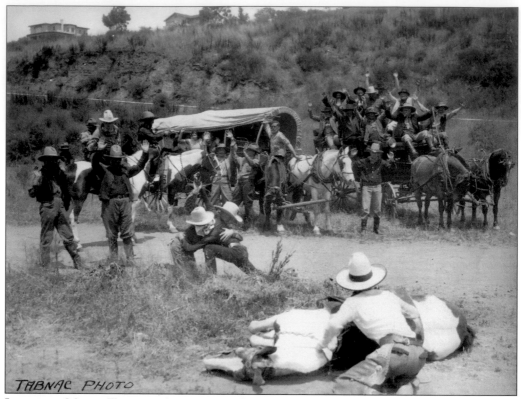

TABNAC PHOTO

INCEVILLE MOVIE FILMING. Actors are performing a scene for a silent western on an Inceville movie set in Santa Monica Canyon, c. 1912. (Courtesy Marc Wanamaker/Bison Archives.)

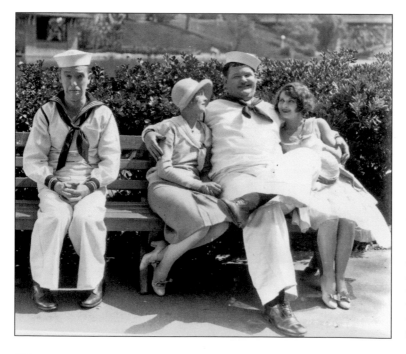

LAUREL AND HARDY. One of the greatest comedy teams, Laurel and Hardy are pictured here in a scene from one of the many movies they appeared in together. They first teamed up in 1926 at the Hal Roach Studios and starred in more than a 100 motion pictures. Stan Laurel lived in Santa Monica for many years. His last years were spent at the Oceana Hotel on Ocean Avenue.

SHIRLEY TEMPLE. Shirley Temple was born in Santa Monica in 1928 and became one of the most famous child performers in the world. She appeared in her first movie at the age of three and was one of the highest-paid stars in Hollywood. Some of her best-known films are *Heidi* and *Rebecca of Sunnybrook Farm*. In 1969, Temple was appointed a U.S. representative to the United Nations General Assembly. (Courtesy Marc Wanamaker/Bison Archives.)

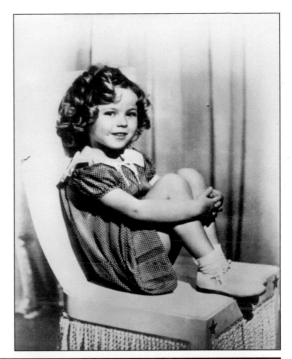

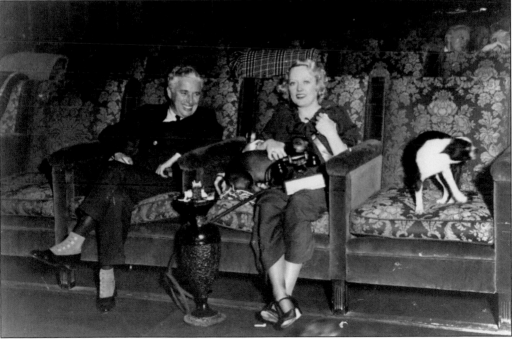

CHAPLIN AND DAVIES. Actor Charlie Chaplin and actress Marion Davies are pictured in the screening room of the Hearst Castle in San Simeon. The Moorish castle was built by William Randolph Hearst on 127 acres. It had 165 rooms. Hearst also built an estate in the late 1920s for his mistress Marion Davies. There were more than 100 rooms and 37 fireplaces in the main house. There were four guest houses on the original estate, plus a building to accommodate the large staff. (Courtesy Marc Wanamaker/Bison Archives.)

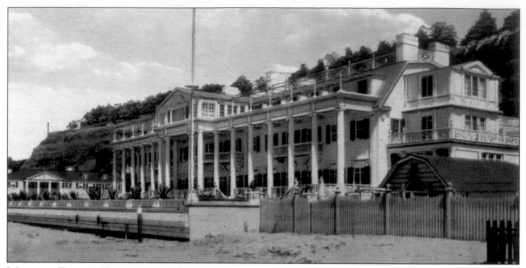

MARION DAVIES ESTATE, 415 PACIFIC COAST HIGHWAY. In 1926, William Randolph Hearst, a newspaper magnate, began development of the most extravagant home along the Gold Coast—the Marion Davies estate. It spanned five acres. In 1945, due to ill health, Davies sold the mansion to a private party, who converted it to a hotel and health club. The state purchased the property in 1960 and leased it to the City of Santa Monica. The existing structure, the guest house on the far left, was damaged in the 1994 Northridge earthquake. A generous gift from the Annenberg Foundation has made it possible, under a tri-party agreement between the city, the state, and the Annenberg Foundation, to preserve the location as a public beach facility. (Courtesy Bison Archives.)

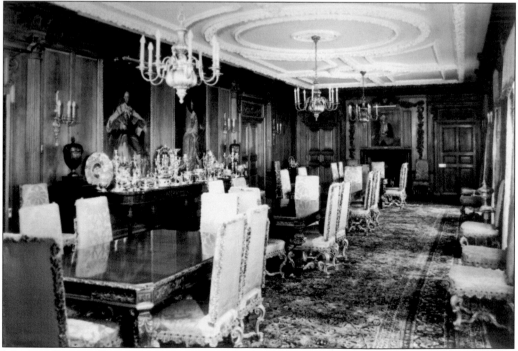

MARION DAVIES ESTATE INTERIOR, 1930S. This photograph shows the elegant dining room in the Davies estate. Most of the furnishings in the house were imported from Europe. (Courtesy Marc Wanamaker/Bison Archives.)

MARY PICKFORD. Silent-screen star Mary Pickford lived in Santa Monica on the Gold Coast with her husband, Douglas Fairbanks. She is pictured here on her wedding day, March 28, 1920. Pickford won an Oscar for *Coquette* in 1929. (Courtesy Marc Wanamaker/Bison Archives.)

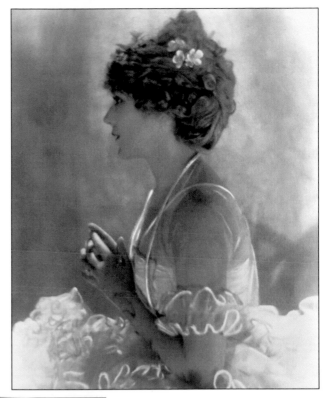

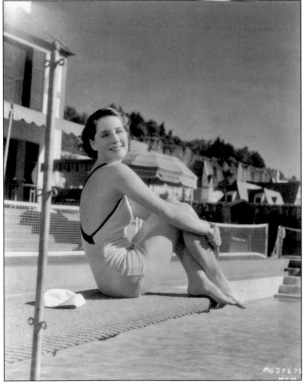

NORMA SHEARER, FILM ACTRESS AT HER GOLD COAST BEACH HOUSE IN 1929. The Oscar-winning actress performed as a society lady in most of her MGM films. One of her very popular films was *Curtain Call*. Shearer loved opera. She and her husband, Irving Thalberg, in later years sold their beach house to Barron Hilton. (Courtesy Marc Wanamaker/Bison Archives.)

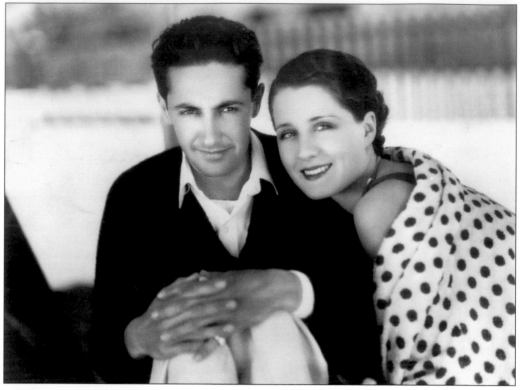

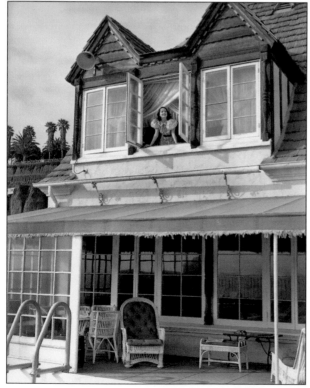

IRVING THALBERG AND NORMA SHEARER. In 1929, Thalberg and Shearer are pictured at their Gold Coast house, designed by architect John Byers. Thalberg was head of Universal Studios at the age of 20 and supervisor of production for MGM at 25. He and Shearer were married in 1927. (Courtesy Marc Wanamaker/Bison Archives.)

MERLE OBERON, 1938. The actress is looking at the ocean view from her Gold Coast home. (Courtesy Marc Wanamaker/Bison Archives.)

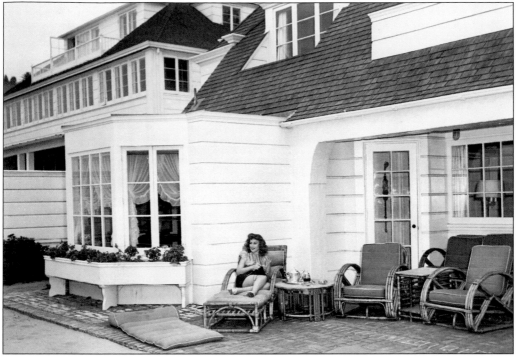

PAULETTE GODDARD, 1945. The actress is pictured sitting on the patio of her Gold Coast beach house. (Courtesy Marc Wanamaker/Bison Archives.)

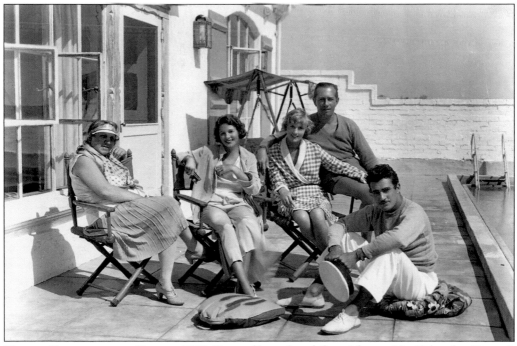

NORMA TALMADGE AND FAMILY, 1929. Pictured here, from left to right, are Mrs. Talmadge, Norma's mother; Norma; Constance and her husband, Townsend Netcher; and Gilbert Roland gathering on the patio of Norma's Gold Coast home. (Courtesy Marc Wanamaker/Bison Archives.)

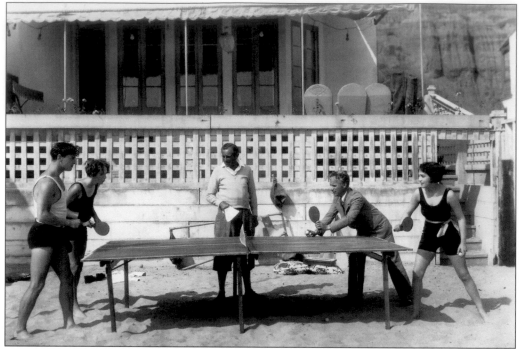

BEBE DANIELS GOLD COAST BEACH HOUSE, 1928. The group of four playing table tennis, from left to right, are Dick Hyland, Norma Talmadge, Charles Chaplin, and Bebe Daniels. Daniels made several movies at Paramount Studio and was a renowned aviator. (Courtesy Marc Wanamaker/Bison Archives.)

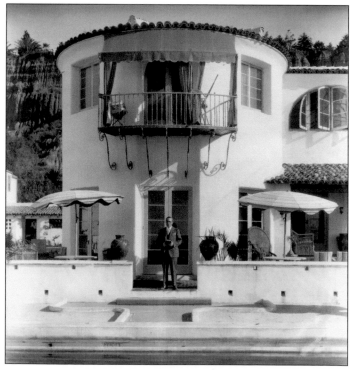

LOUIS B. MAYER, 1928. Mayer stands in front of his Gold Coast beach house at 237 Palisades Beach Road. He was one of the founders and the head of Metro-Goldwyn-Mayer, the largest motion-picture studio in the country. (Courtesy Marc Wanamaker/ Bison Archives.)

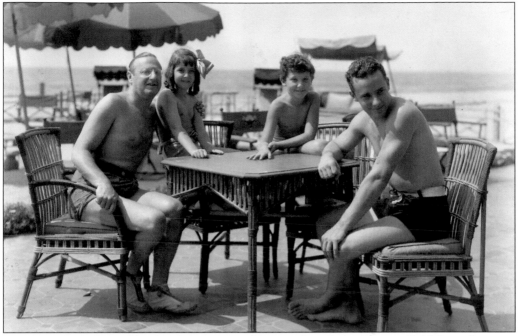

JESSE LASKY. Lasky and his family are pictured here at their Santa Monica Gold Coast home in 1929. He was the head of Paramount Studios. (Courtesy Marc Wanamaker/Bison Archives.)

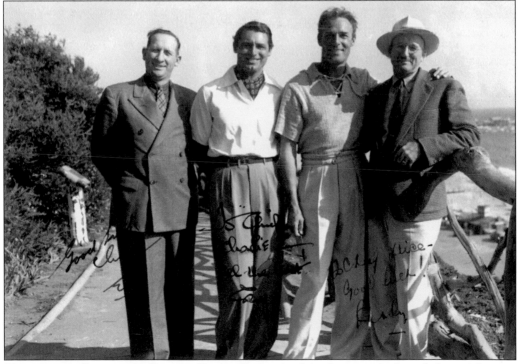

CELEBRITIES POSE WITH POLICE CHIEF. Posing in this photograph, from left to right, are unidentified, Cary Grant, Randolph Scott, and police chief Charles Dice, *c.* 1940. Grant and Scott's home was on the Gold Coast.

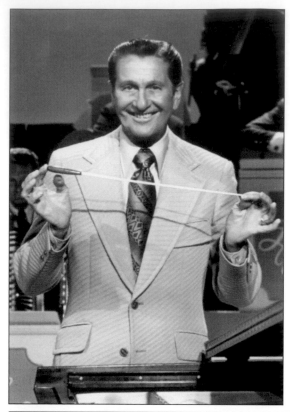

LAWRENCE WELK. In 1938, the Welk Band debuted at a hotel on New Year's Eve where the name "Champagne Music of Lawrence Welk" was born. In 1951, the band appeared at the Aragon Ballroom at Lick Pier and was such a hit that it debuted on national television with the Lennon Sisters. Welk retired in 1982 after 58 years of entertaining. Welk lived in Santa Monica, where he died in 1992. (Courtesy Welk Syndication.)

MILES PLAYHOUSE. This Spanish Colonial Revival building was constructed in 1929 by John Byers, one of the city's prominent architects. In his last will and testament, J. Euclid Miles, a former city councilman, bequeathed to the city $25,000 to erect a public recreation hall for young men and women as a memorial to his wife, Mary. The playhouse is located in Reed Park (formerly Lincoln Park). It was designated a city landmark in 1975. (Santa Monica Historical Society Museum, Bill Beebe Collection.)

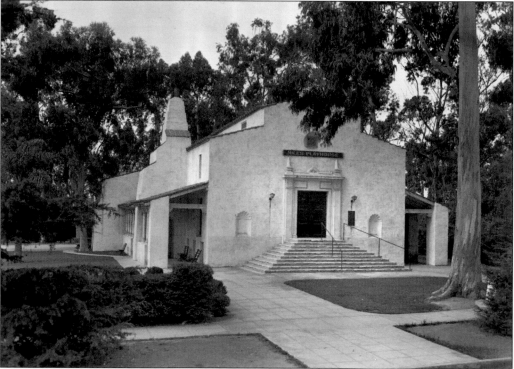

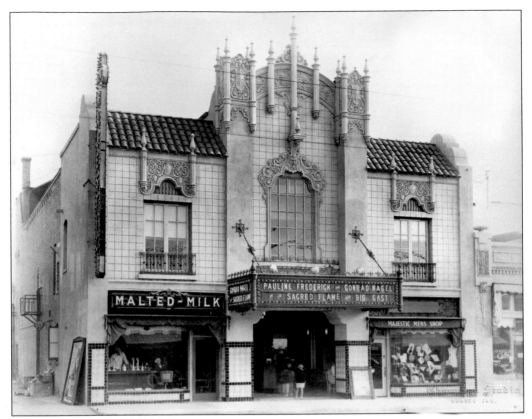

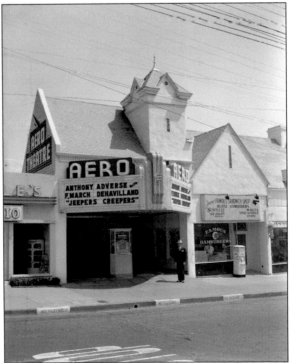

MAJESTIC THEATER, 1911. Now called the Mayfair Theater, it was built by Charles Tegner and designed by architect Henry C. Hollwedel, who also designed Henshey's Department Store, which was owned by Tegner. The theater is currently owned by Karl Schober, grandson of Tegner, and is located at 214 Santa Monica Boulevard. (Courtesy Virginia Tegner Spurgin.)

AERO THEATER. Located at 1382 Montana Avenue, the theater and its adjacent stores were constructed by Donald W. Douglas, an aviation pioneer, in 1939. It was designed by architect P. M. Woolpert in the French Norman style. The theater was open seven nights per week during World War II so Douglas factory workers could catch a flick whenever they finished their shift. (Santa Monica Historical Society Museum, Bill Beebe Collection.)

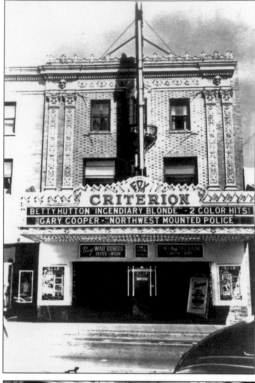

CRITERION THEATER. The theater, a reinforced concrete building, was built in 1923. Part of the land on which the theater is constructed was the site of the original Presbyterian church built in 1887. The theater is located on the Third Street Promenade at Arizona Avenue. (Santa Monica Historical Society Museum, *Outlook* Collection.)

EL MIRO THEATER. Now named the Cine Theater, the theater is located at 1443 Third Street Promenade. Built in 1934 during the Depression, it was designed by architect Norman Alpaugh. The theater is constructed on the site of the former Evening Outlook Building. (Santa Monica Historical Society Museum, Bill Beebe Collection.)

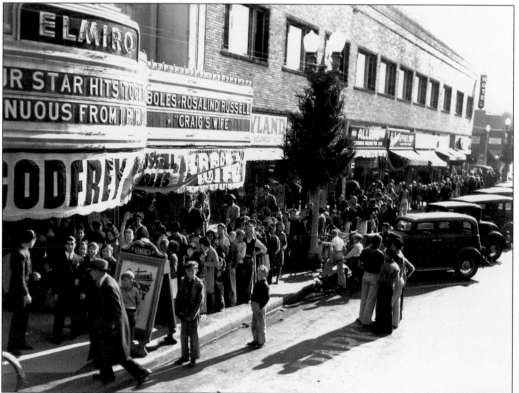

Nine

DONALD DOUGLAS AND WORLD WAR II

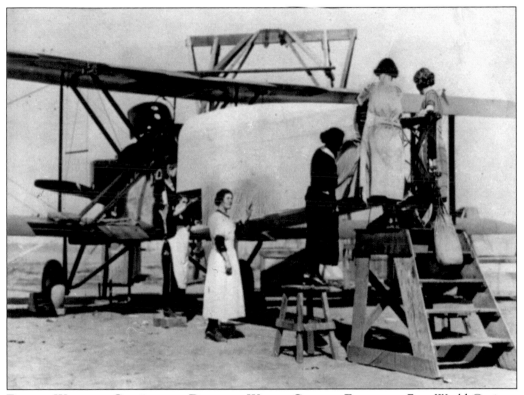

FEMALE WORKERS COVERING A DOUGLAS WORLD CRUISER FUSELAGE. Four World Cruisers made the first round-the-world flight. The son of a New York banker, Donald W. Douglas was born in Brooklyn on April 6, 1892. As a boy, he built and flew model airplanes. While at Annapolis, he saw the Wright Brothers demonstrate the first airplane purchased by the United States Army. The Douglas planes of the round-the-world flight in 1924 attracted men and women from around the world to Santa Monica. In 1929, 20 female pilots, including Amelia Earhart, gathered at Clover Field for the start of the first women's cross-country air race. The race brought fame to the female pilots and national attention to Santa Monica. During World War II, the Douglas plant operated three shifts a day, seven days a week. Gen. Dwight Eisenhower declared that the Douglas C-47 planes were one of the key weapons used to win the war. (Santa Monica Historical Society Museum, *Outlook* Collection.)

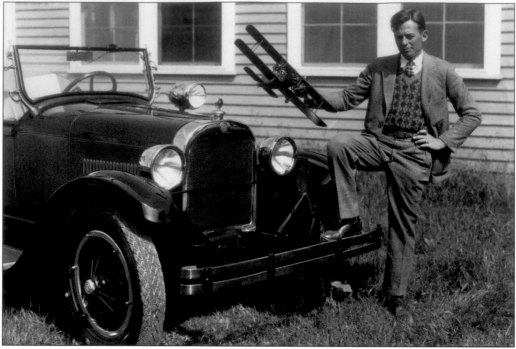

DONALD W. DOUGLAS. The aviation pioneer established the Douglas Aircraft Company in 1922 at Wilshire Boulevard and Chelsea Avenue (named Douglas Park in 1936). His Douglas cruisers made the first round-the-world flight. Douglas Aircraft built many airplanes for the armed forces and became Santa Monica's largest employer throughout the 1940s and 1950s.

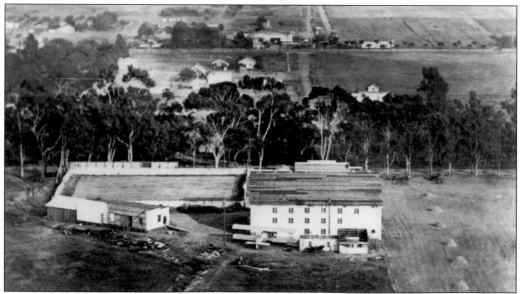

DOUGLAS AIRCRAFT COMPANY. The site, originally a reservoir owned by the Santa Monica Land and Water Company, was bought by the city in 1917. The land was used for a movie studio before being leased to the Douglas Aircraft Company. It was here that the four "round-the-world" air cruisers were built and moved to Clover Field for their historic flight in 1924. Douglas Aircraft Company occupied the site until 1929, when it moved to its new Ocean Park plant.

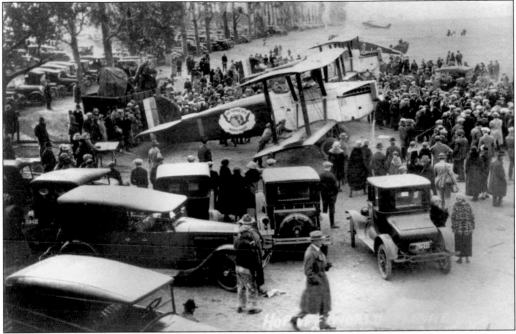

WORLD CRUISER TAKES OFF. One of the four Douglas World Cruisers is pictured here just before taking off on the round-the-world flight from Clover Field in Santa Monica on March 17, 1924.

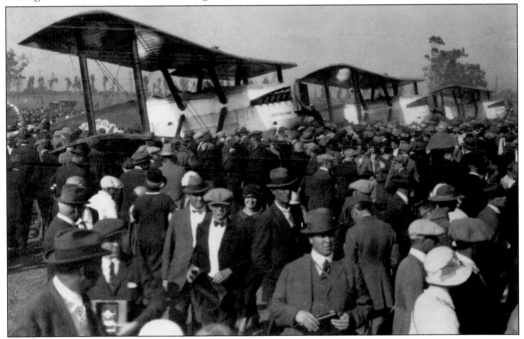

WORLD CRUISER RETURNS. Crowds at Clover Field Airport greet the World Cruisers on their return from the six-month, round-the-world flight. Clover Field, first known in 1923 as Santa Monica Flying Field, was renamed in honor of Lt. G. Clover, an army flyer from Los Angeles who was killed in France in World War I. The city purchased the airport in 1926. It was renamed Santa Monica Airport. (Santa Monica Historical Society Museum, *Outlook* Collection.)

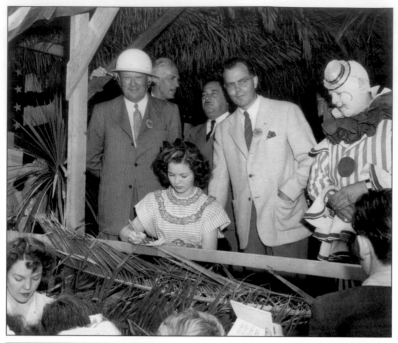

SHIRLEY TEMPLE ASSISTS WITH WAR EFFORT, 1940s. Child movie star Shirley Temple, born in Santa Monica in 1928, is pictured here signing war bonds to aid in the country's World War II effort. (Santa Monica Historical Society Museum, *Outlook* Collection.)

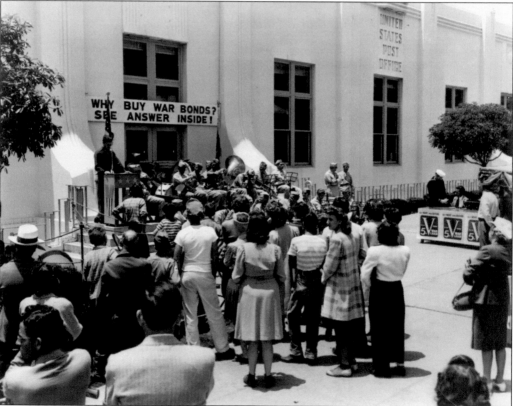

BUY WAR BONDS, 1941. War bonds were sold at the Santa Monica Post Office to help the war effort.

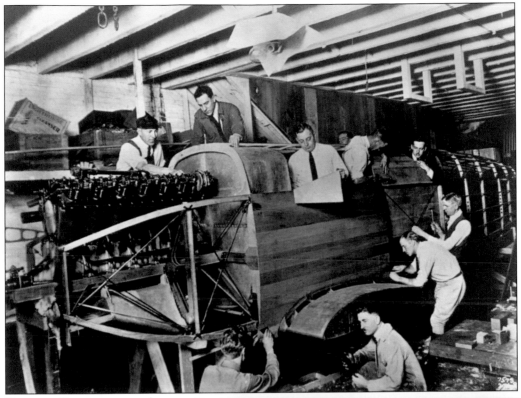

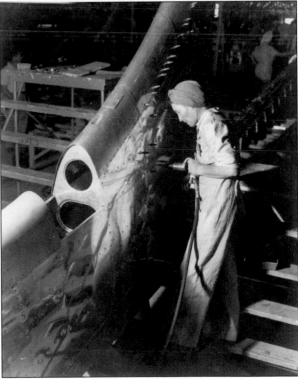

DONALD DOUGLAS AND AIRCRAFT WORKERS C. 1924. Donald Douglas, pictured here with some of his employees, works on a Cloudster at his aircraft company. (Santa Monica Historical Society Museum, *Outlook* Collection.)

ROSIE THE RIVETER, EARLY 1940S. Pictured here is a female worker on the job. During the war, half of the work force in the Douglas Aircraft Company plant were women.

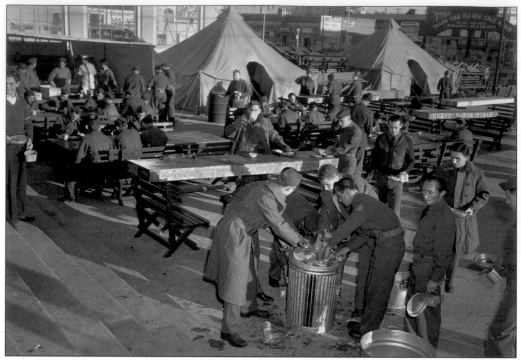

THE 144TH ARTILLERY HEADQUARTERS AT THEIR ENCAMPMENT IN OCEAN PARK DURING WORLD WAR II. When the war started, the harbor foghorn was mounted on top of city hall and was used to broadcast air-raid warnings. Civilians reported for duty as air-raid wardens. (Santa Monica Historical Society Museum, Bill Beebe Collection.)

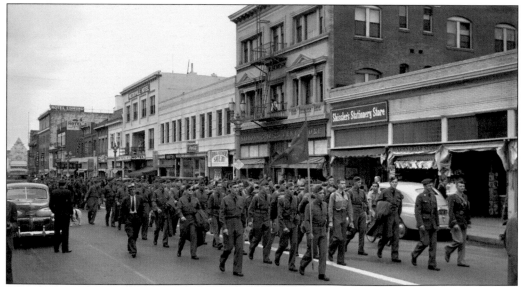

WORLD WAR II VOLUNTEERS, 1941. Army volunteers entrain for duty from Ocean Park where they were encamped. Other army groups manning antiaircraft gun emplacements, encamped at various open fields throughout the Westside. Additional antiaircraft batteries were set up at Cloverfield Avenue to guard the camouflaged Douglas Aircraft plant that from the air resembled a housing tract. (Santa Monica Historical Society Museum, Bill Beebe Collection.)

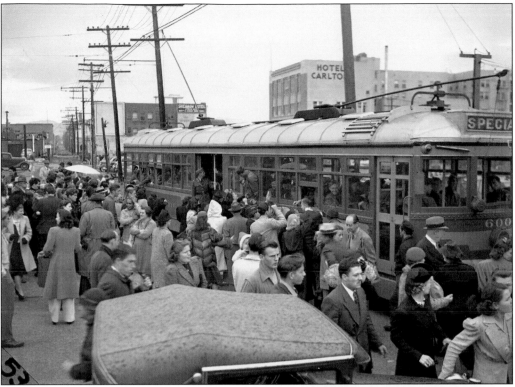

**WORLD WAR II SEND-OFF,
1941.** Crowds bid farewell to army
volunteers leaving for duty from
their encampment in Ocean Park.
(Santa Monica Historical Society
Museum, Bill Beebe Collection.)

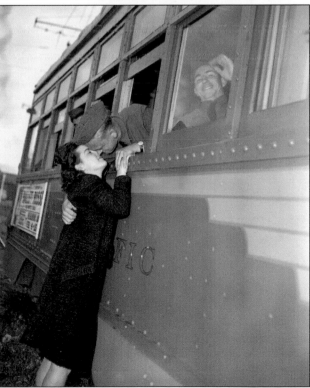

**A GOODBYE KISS AS ARMY
VOLUNTEER GOES OFF TO DUTY,
1941.** This was a familiar scene
during World War II. (Santa
Monica Historical Society
Museum, Bill Beebe Collection.)

DISCOVER THOUSANDS OF LOCAL HISTORY BOOKS FEATURING MILLIONS OF VINTAGE IMAGES

Arcadia Publishing, the leading local history publisher in the United States, is committed to making history accessible and meaningful through publishing books that celebrate and preserve the heritage of America's people and places.

Find more books like this at
www.arcadiapublishing.com

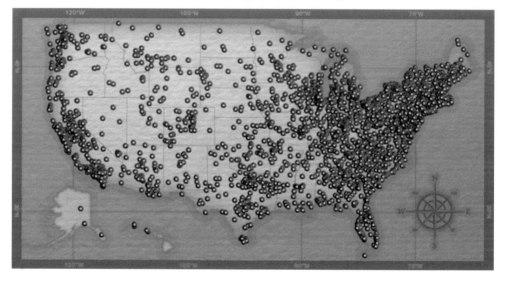

Search for your hometown history, your old stomping grounds, and even your favorite sports team.

Consistent with our mission to preserve history on a local level, this book was printed in South Carolina on American-made paper and manufactured entirely in the United States. Products carrying the accredited Forest Stewardship Council (FSC) label are printed on 100 percent FSC-certified paper.

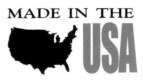

MADE IN THE USA